Dad

Merry christmas 2007.

Love

Mark + Grace.

Scotland's Great Ships

Scotland's Great Ships

BRIAN D. OSBORNE
and
RONALD ARMSTRONG

Luath Press Limited
EDINBURGH
www.luath.co.uk

First published 2007

ISBN (10): 1-906307-04-0
ISBN (13): 978-1-906307-04-2

The paper used in this book is recyclable. It is made from
low-chlorine pulps produced in a low-energy, low-emission manner from
renewable forests.

Printed and bound by
CPI Antony Rowe, Chippenham

Typeset in 11 point Sabon
by 3btype.com

For Anne Armstrong

Contents

List of Illustrations   ix
Colour Plate Section   xiii
Acknowledgements   xvii
Map   xviii
Map Key   xix

CHAPTER 1   Scotland's Ships: in search of the iconic   1
CHAPTER 2   Scotland's Earliest Ships   20
CHAPTER 3   *Great Michael*   28
CHAPTER 4   Emigrant Ships   34
CHAPTER 5   PS *Comet*   44
CHAPTER 6   PS *Britannia*   55
CHAPTER 7   The Puffer   68
CHAPTER 8   HMS *Black Prince*   73
CHAPTER 9   *Cutty Sark*   81
CHAPTER 10   *Glenlee* and Other Clyde Veterans   93
CHAPTER 11   RRS *Discovery* and *Scotia*   101
CHAPTER 12   *Lusitania*   113
CHAPTER 13   HMS *Hood*   128
CHAPTER 14   The *Queen Mary* and the Last of the Liners   139
CHAPTER 15   HMS *Vanguard*   153
CHAPTER 16   PS *Waverley*   161
CHAPTER 17   RY *Britannia*   172

Appendix   179
Timeline   185
Glossary   187
Index   193

List of Illustrations

FIG. 1.1   Shipping on the Clyde. A late 19th century view of Glasgow Harbour with a characteristic mix of steam and sailing ships.

FIG. 1.2   *Hindustan*. One of the Irrawaddy Flotilla Company's ships trading in Burma.

FIG. 1.3   Robert Napier. The father of Clyde Shipbuilding portrayed around the time of his first Cunard contract.

FIG. 1.4   Admiral Duncan. The victor of the Battle of Camperdown.

FIG. 1.5   Admiral Keith. One of the many distinguished Scottish admirals of the period.

FIG. 1.6   HMS *Unicorn*. The veteran frigate now preserved at Dundee.

FIG. 1.7   *Shamrock III*. One of Thomas Lipton's line of unsuccessful challengers for the America's Cup.

FIG. 2.1   Birlinn Drawing. The characteristic ship of the West Highlands in the medieval and early modern period. Image based on tomb at Rodel, Harris.

FIG. 2.2   Gokstad Ship. The magnificent vessel preserved in Oslo's Vikingskipshuset.

FIG. 3.1   James IV. The Royal inspiration behind the *Michael*.

FIG. 4.1   *Columbia*. The Anchor Line ship traded between Scotland, Ireland and New York carrying many emigrants.

FIG. 4.2   *Metagama*. The Canadian Pacific ship noted for its role in emigration from the Western Isles.

FIG. 5.1   *Comet*. Europe's first commercially successful steamship and the foundation of a Clydeside tradition.

FIG. 5.2   Henry Bell. The talented, if financially unstable, owner and designer of the *Comet*.

FIG. 6.1   *Britannia* in ice at Boston. The first Cunarder being cut free from an iced-up Boston Harbour.

FIG. 6.2   Charles Dickens. Portrayed at around the age of his January crossing to America in *Britannia*.

FIG. 7.1   The puffer *Saxon* at Millport 1965.

FIG. 8.1   HMS *Black Prince* photographed after her 1875 refit.

FIG. 9.1   A pre-First World War photo of *Cutty Sark* lying at Falmouth.

FIG. 10.1   *Glenlee*'s bell.

FIG. 10.2   *Glenlee*'s figurehead.

FIG. 11.1   *Discovery*. The veteran of Antarctic exploration preserved in the city where she was built.

FIG. 11.2   *Scotia*. SY *Scotia* trapped in the Weddell Sea at 74 degrees 1 minute south.

FIG. 12.1   *Lusitania* from a pre First World War postcard.

FIG. 12.2   An artist's impression by Charles Nixon of the sinking of the *Lusitania*.

FIG. 13.1   HMS *Hood* leaving the fitting out basin at John Brown's.

FIG. 14.1   *Queen Mary* interior – the art deco style of her original design.

FIG. 14.2   *Queen Mary* converted to a troop-ship. The crowded accommodation contrasts with pre-war luxury.

FIG. 15.1   HMS *Vanguard* at sea. Britain's last battleship photographed from the deck of a British aircraft carrier.

FIG. 16.1   *Waverley*. The last sea-going paddle steamer.

FIG. 16.2   Steamers at Glasgow. A characteristic view of steamers at the Broomielaw. The left-hand ship is the *Ivanhoe*.

FIG. 16.3   The pioneering turbine steamer *King Edward*.

FIG. 16.4   An earlier *Waverley* – an early photograph of *Waverley III*.

FIG. 17.1   *Royal Yacht Britannia* – dining room.

FIG. 17.2   *Royal Yacht Britannia* – bridge.

Colour Plate Section

FIG. A   Steamboat on the Clyde. A lithograph from William Daniell's *A Voyage Around Great Britain*. The picture, done in 1817, just five years after the *Comet's* first voyage, depicts one of the first generation of Clyde steamers off Dumbarton. *Authors' Collection*

FIG. B   *Aquitania*. An early postcard of the classic four-funnelled Cunard liner in New York harbour. *Aquitania* was built at Clydebank in 1913 and went into service in May 1914. She was slower than the *Lusitania* but was renowned as the 'ship beautiful'. After a long career she was broken up at Faslane on the Gareloch in 1950. *Authors' Collection*

FIG. C   *Hector*. A full scale replica of the Dutch-built emigrant ship that took 200 Highland migrants from Loch Broom to Nova Scotia in 1773. She forms the centrepiece of the Hector Heritage Quay in Pictou, Nova Scotia. *Pictou Antigonish Regional Library*

FIG. D   *Comet*. Henry Bell's advertisement for the *Comet* promised that it would sail by the power of wind, air and steam and this illustration shows the large square sail rigged on the funnel. It is interesting to compare the funnel in this illustration with that in 5.1. *Authors' Collection*

FIG. E   *Britannia*. The first Cunarder into service, the paddle steamer *Britannia* as depicted by the noted American marine artist Samuel Ward Stanton (1870–1912). Stanton was a passenger on the maiden voyage of the *Titanic* in 1912. He boarded her at Cherbourg and was drowned when she sank. *Mariners Museum, Newport News, Virginia*

FIG. F   *Black Prince & Warrior*. A late 19th century painting of Britain's first two iron-clad ships by Charles Nixon. The two ships were from the same design but for some reason *Warrior* was always slightly faster than the Napier-built *Black Prince*. *Warrior* is preserved today at Portsmouth, *Black Prince*, after a long career and several name-changes, was scrapped in 1923. *Authors' Collection*

FIG. G   *Cutty Sark*. Alone of the classic Scottish clippers *Cutty Sark* has been saved and now sits at Greenwich – a setting remote from her birthplace on the Leven and the wool quays of Australia but one of undoubted grandeur and relevance. *Cutty Sark Trust*

FIG. H   *Glenlee*. After a long and varied career the *Glenlee* has returned to the river of her birth and to a secure future in the care of the Clyde Maritime Trust. This view shows her in her current berth at Yorkhill Quay. *Jim Ramsay*

FIG. I   *Discovery*. After a long career in Polar exploration, including Scott's 1901 expedition to the Antarctic, *Discovery* now forms the central feature of Dundee's Discovery Quay and plays a central role in the city's image. *VisitScotland Angus & Dundee*

FIG. J   HMS *Hood* in the Pacific. An aerial shot of the 'mighty *Hood*' taken when she was on her round the world cruise in 1923/24 as part of the Special Service Squadron. Note the flag of Vice Admiral Sir Frederick Field flying from the mainmast. US *Naval Historical Center*

FIG. K   *Queen Mary* in war-time paint. The luxury Cunarder in war-time camouflage lying at the Tail of the Bank off Greenock. Notice the fleet of attendant vessels alongside. She has presumably just completed one of her high-speed transatlantic crossings bringing thousands of Allied soldiers to the UK. *Imperial War Museum, A25909*

FIG. L   Launch of the puffer *Briton*. The Kirkintilloch shipbuilding yard of J. & J. Hay launched the *Briton* in 1893. The restricted width of the Forth and Clyde Canal made a side launch rather than the traditional stern-first launch a necessity. *East Dunbartonshire Libraries*

FIG. M   HMS *Vanguard* at high speed. An impressive view of *Vanguard* steaming at 30 knots on a high speed run during a NATO exercise in September 1952. US *Naval Historical Centre*

FIG. N   Paddle Steamer *Helensburgh*. Built by the renowned Dumbarton shipbuilder William Denny and engined by Robert Napier, *Helensburgh* was one of the fastest steamers of her day. *Authors' Collection*

FIG. O   Paddle Steamer *Waverley*. Photographed off Campbeltown, the *Waverley* continues the Clyde steamer tradition of the *Comet* and *Helensburgh*. *Waverley Excursions*

FIG. P   *Sir Walter Scott*. A delightful vintage view of the Loch Katrine steamer *Sir Walter Scott* – named in tribute to the great author's popularisation of the Trossachs area in poems such as 'Lady of the Lake' and novels like *Rob Roy*. *Authors' Collection*

FIG. Q   *Royal Yacht Britannia*. Very much the last of a line and a fitting testament to the skills and craftsmanship that made 'Clyde Built' a by-word for quality, even if this product of the Clyde has had to find a final home on the Forth. *Royal Yacht Britannia*

Acknowledgements

The many institutions and individuals who have provided illustrations for this work are acknowledged beside each illustration but it is our pleasure to acknowledge the particularly enthusiastic help and assistance afforded by Susie Barratt (Comunn Birlinn); Lucy Caldwell (Royal Yacht *Britannia)*; Graham Hopner (West Dunbartonshire Libraries); Fern MacDonald (Pictou Antigonish Regional Library); Louise Massara (*Cutty Sark* Trust); David Munro (Royal Scottish Geographical Society); Jim Ramsay (Clyde Maritime Trust); Nicola Reid *(Waverley* Excursions); Roderick Stewart (*Unicorn* Preservation Society) and Seth White.

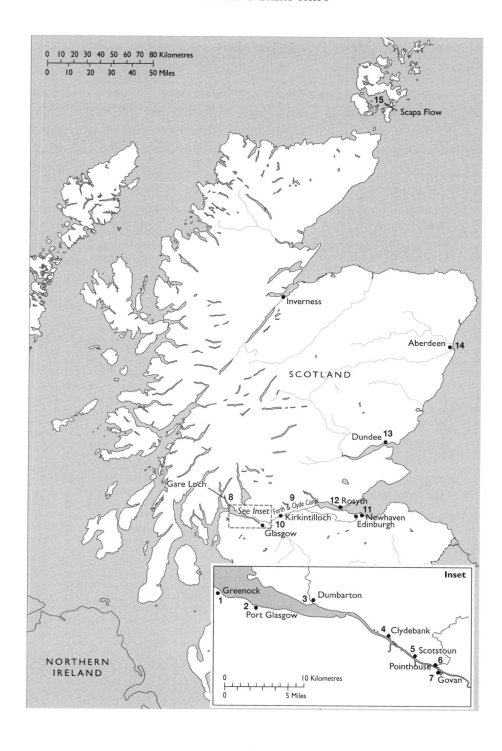

0 10 20 30 40 50 60 70 80 Kilometres

0 10 20 30 40 50 Miles

15
Scapa Flow

Inverness

Aberdeen **14**

SCOTLAND

Dundee **13**

Gare Loch

8
See Inset
Forth & Clyde Canal
9
Kirkintilloch
10
Glasgow
12 Rosyth
11
Newhaven
Edinburgh

NORTHERN
IRELAND

Inset

Greenock
1
2
Port Glasgow
3 Dumbarton
4 Clydebank
5 Scotstoun
Pointhouse
6
7 Govan

0   10 Kilometres

0   5 Miles

MAP OF PRINCIPAL LOCATIONS

1. Greenock – Robert Duncan's yard launched the Cunarder *Britannia*

2. Port Glasgow – Important 19th century shipbuilding centre. John Wood's yard built the *Comet* and the Cunarder *Acadia* while A. Rodger's yard launched *Glenlee*, Russell & Co. built *Falls of Clyde* and William Hamilton's yard built *Moshulu*

3. Dumbarton – Birthplace of *Cutty Sark*, started by Scott & Linton, completed by William Denny. *Sir Walter Scott* was also built by Denny

4. Clydebank – John Brown's yard was the birthplace of many of the greatest ships of Scotland, including *Lusitania*, HMS *Hood*, *Queen Mary*, *Queen Elizabeth*, HMS *Vanguard*, Royal Yacht *Britannia*, & *Queen Elizabeth 2*

5. Scotstoun – Charles Connell's yard built *Balclutha*

6. Pointhouse – A. & J. Inglis, the builders of *Waverley*, was just one of the many yards actually in Glasgow

7. Govan – The pioneering iron-shipbuilding yard of Robert Napier, 'Father of Clyde ship-building', launched HMS *Black Prince*

8. Gare Loch – World War 2 naval base and post-war shipbreaking yard

9. Kirkintilloch – The Kirkintilloch yards of J. & J. Hay and P. MacGregor were the birthplace of many puffers

10. Forth & Clyde Canal – the Forth & Clyde Canal was the major water-route for transport of goods and people across central Scotland throughout the 19th century

11. Newhaven – James IV's great warship *Michael* was built on the shores of the Forth

12. Rosyth – Major naval base in First World War

13. Dundee – Centre of whaler building and birthplace of *Discovery* and *Terra Nova*

14. Aberdeen – Home of many famous clippers including *Thermopylae*

15. Scapa Flow – Major naval base in two world wars

CHAPTER I

Scotland's Ships:
in search of the iconic

> We got close enough to touch the big ships that pass
> where the Clyde runs narrow and deep. We knew them
> all... They were OUR ships. Their engine rooms were
> manned by OUR uncles and brothers and cousins.
>
> Tom Gallacher: *Hunting Shadows*[1]

TO ATTEMPT TO cover all of Scotland's ships in one volume would clearly
be an overambitious exercise, and even if we limited it to 'Great Ships'
(whatever and however they may be defined) we would be likely to produce an unmanageable volume and one of limited interest to that elusive
creature, the general reader.

We have been much more selective and confined our attention to those
ships which have something to say to us today and which represent more
than just themselves – ships which in some way can be seen as Scottish
icons. It would be hard to deny this iconic status to 'celebrity' ships like
the *Queen Mary* (Chapter 14) or HMS *Hood* (Chapter 13), but it is as
valid a description of lesser-known vessels like the first Cunarder, the little
paddle steamer *Britannia* (Chapter 6). Some ships are included, like the
Britannia, or the *Comet* (Chapter 5), because of what they started; others,
like HMS *Vanguard* (Chapter 15), because they are the last of their line.
Other entries cover those ships with a special place in the Scottish imagination – the puffer (Chapter 7), for example, or the Clyde pleasure
steamer, exemplified by the last survivor, the paddle steamer *Waverley*
(Chapter 16). We have shown a certain preference for ships that survived,
even if they are in themselves perhaps, in reality, unremarkable – the
Glenlee (Chapter 10) could be seen as a run-of-the-mill ship which has

---

[1] Gallacher, Tom, *Hunting Shadows*, Craig M. Jeffrey, Helensburgh, 1981

achieved iconic status by surviving to our day while their many similar, equally quotidian, contemporaries have long since vanished from the seas and public awareness. Some survivors are, of course, far from run-of-the-mill – never a description which could have been applied to the majestic *Queen Mary* or the heartstoppingly beautiful *Cutty Sark* (Chapter 9) – surely one of the most graceful craft ever to put to sea.

It is also appropriate to admit that our selection has in some cases been unashamedly idiosyncratic and reflects themes and ships that speak particularly loudly to us, our prejudices and imaginations.

Analysis of the contents will show a bias towards the products of the Clyde, and the fact that both authors were born and raised by the banks of that great river may be assumed to account for this partiality. This would, in fact, be untrue. The Clyde is so central to the story of the Scottish ship that even the most devoted partisan of the Dundee whaler or the Aberdeen clipper would be hard put to compile a book greatly differing in balance from ours. It was the Clyde that saw the birth of the Scottish tradition of steamship building and marine engineering – from the *Comet*'s first voyage of 1812 to the latest high-tech warship to slip down the ways at the Scotstoun yard of BAE Systems, the story of the modern ship and the Clyde have been interwoven.

While the Clyde in 2007 is sadly reduced from its glory years when the river was lined with yards from Rutherglen to Greenock – today less than a handful of yards at Govan, Scotstoun and Port Glasgow maintain the great tradition – nevertheless, the primacy of the Clyde demands that any book on Scotland's Great Ships is heavily Clyde-weighted.

In the 150 years between the *Comet*'s first voyage and the mid 20th century, around 30,000 ships were launched on the Clyde. The Scottish writer Neil Munro in his 1907 travelogue *Clyde, River and Firth*[2] could, writing at perhaps the peak of the Clyde's success, refer to the Clyde as the 'Ship Shop'. Writing of her ships he observed:

> They are found in the oddest waters; they have been taken by the Kara Sea and the Yenisei River to Lake Baikal in the heart of Asia; in parts, like nursery picture-blocks, they have been put together on the inland seas of North America... Clyde clippers have broken records and held them long in the days of the 'wind-jammer', when

---

[2] Munro, Neil, *The Clyde, River and Firth*, A&C Black, London, 1907

each trip from China or Australia was a feverish race, and Clyde steamers, since the marine engine came to being, have had a *cachet* like Sheffield cutlery or the buns of Bath, so that praise of them is a convention of English literature, and Kipling and Conrad, voicing the sentiments of the seaman, credit their heroic ships, their shrewdest engineers, to the Clyde.

'Trade followed the Flag' – so went the old imperial maxim. Many Scottish ships built in Victorian and Edwardian times were like bands of iron that held the British Empire together – bands of trade and of administration. In particular, the enormously important routes of the Raj that in the 19th and 20th centuries brought mercantile and military reinforcement to the Indian sub-continent, had a natural extension in the huge river delta of India's neighbour, Burma. This, the world's sixth largest river system, needed a specially evolved and perfected genre of shipping and it was largely provided by the mother country's shipbuilding industry.

FIG. 1.1
Shipping on the Clyde. A late 19th century view of Glasgow Harbour with a characteristic mix of steam and sailing ships.
Authors' Collection

Most of the Burmese fleet was built on the banks of another, colder river, thousands of miles away. The Scottish shipbuilding yards on the Clyde saw the building of scores of ships that were designed with Burmese conditions in mind. The coastal and deep-sea vessels that took goods and supplies, and civil servants, merchant company employees and military men, out from the old country, had been built within a few miles or even a few hundred yards of each other; in fact, at one time a majority of them had been constructed on the slips of the Denny shipbuilding family's shipyard at Dumbarton. The fleet was run as a joint enterprise by Denny and another Scottish company, Paddy Henderson, and collectively known as the Irrawaddy Flotilla Company. In addition, the same Scottish yards built the shallow draught vessels that plied the muddy waters of the mighty Irrawaddy and its tributary streams like the Chindwin, and carried people and goods up-country.

Something in the order of 450 such vessels were sent out to the East, usually in prefabricated form. Most were paddlers, some stern-wheelers, Mississippi-style, as well as the more familiar Clyde estuary type. Lastly, the market for support vessels like dredgers and specialist ships that brought the rich Burma oil (as well as teak and other raw materials) to European markets was more often than not met by the Clyde. As an intriguing footnote, many years later in the 1950s an experimental form of hovercraft was developed by Denny as a new generation of vessels, also intended for the broad shallow rivers of the Orient but never delivered.

The heyday of the hybrid shipping company had been, however, in the years before the Second World War; or perhaps it was a generation earlier, when Kipling dreamt of:

... the paddles chunkin' from Rangoon to Mandalay.

The eclipse of the 'old flotilla' actually came with the wartime invasion of Burma by Japanese forces, when the entire fleet was scuttled by the British in a maritime 'scorched earth' policy.

Not only was the Clyde by far the greatest centre of shipbuilding in Scotland, but it consistently out-produced the other British shipbuilding areas and made a huge contribution to the world's total output. For much of the 19th and early 20th centuries the UK yards produced over half the world's total shipping tonnage, with the lion's share of this coming from the Clyde. In 1870, for example, the Clyde yards produced 70 per cent of the total British tonnage.

FIG. 1.2

Hindustan. One of the Irrawaddy Flotilla Company's ships trading in Burma.

West Dumbartonshire Libraries

Scotland has long had a close relationship with ships and the sea – for Scots through the ages the sea was not something that divided, but rather something that united. In Chapter 2, dealing with our early ships, we look at the role of the curragh and birlinn in linking the islands and coasts of the west. Equally significant was the role of the ship on the east coast of Scotland, with trading links to Scandinavia, the Baltic and the Low Countries. From the mid 14th century, if not earlier, Scotland had maintained a 'staple port' in the Low Countries where Scottish exports, such as linen, wool and salt, passed through to its final destination and where the interests of Scottish merchants and sailors were protected. This port, located first at Middelburg, later moved to Bruges and then to Veere on Walcheren Island.

With these links it is hardly surprising that many Scots monarchs found their consorts in the kingdoms and principalities around the North Sea, or that such connections have found their way into popular history and literature: the death of the Maid of Norway, heiress to the Scottish Crown and daughter of King Erik of Norway and granddaughter of Alexander III of Scotland, whose death in 1290 plunged Scotland into the Wars of Independence, being a prime example of the first. 'The Ballad of Sir Patrick Spens' retells a similar story, albeit in a multitude of versions. Sir Walter Scott's version in *Minstrelsy of the Scottish Border* makes the Norwegian connection clear:

> To Noroway, to Noroway,
> To Noroway o'er the faem;
> The king's daughter of Noroway,
> 'Tis thou maun bring her hame.

Indeed the very multiplicity of versions, with the Scots Lords variously drowning off Aberdeen and Aberdour, speaks to the emotional resonance of this tale of a doomed sea voyage for the Scottish people. The sea has continued to echo through Scottish literature down the years. The heroic, if bloody, whaling industry was celebrated in ballads like 'The Bonny Ship the *Diamond*',[3] which recall the days when ports on the east coast sent out ships into the Arctic in search of whale oil to keep the lights burning:

---

[3] 'The Bonny Ship the Diamond' quoted in Osborne, Brian D & Armstrong, Ronald, *Echoes of the Sea, Scotland and the Sea, an anthology*, Canongate, Edinburgh, 1998

The *Diamond* is a ship, my lads, for the Davis Strait she's bound,
And the quay it is all garnished with bonny lasses round:
Captain Thompson gives the order to sail the ocean wide,
Where the sun it never sets, my lads, no darkness dims the sky.

> So cheer up my lads, let your heart never fail
> While the bonny ship, the *Diamond*, goes a-fishing for the whale.

Along the quay at Peterhead, the lasses stand aroon,
Wi' their shawls all pulled around them and the saut tears runnin' doon
Don't you weep, my bonny lass, though you be left behind,
For the rose will grow on Greenland's ice before we change our mind.

> So cheer up my lads, let your heart never fail
> While the bonny ship, the *Diamond*, goes a-fishing for the whale.

Here's a health to the *Resolution*, likewise the *Eliza Swan*,
Here's a health to the *Battler* of Montrose and the *Diamond*, ship of
    fame;
We wear the trousers o' the white, and the jackets o' the blue,
When we return to Peterhead, we'll hae sweethearts anoo,

> So cheer up my lads, let your heart never fail
> While the bonny ship, the *Diamond*, goes a-fishing for the whale.

It'll be bricht both day and nicht when the Greenland lads come hame,
Wi' a ship that's fu' of oil, my lads, and money to our name,
We'll make the cradles for to rock, and the blankets for to tear,
And every lass in Peterhead sing, 'Hushabye, my dear'.

In modern times the 19th-century herring fishing of Caithness formed
the theme for Neil Gunn's masterpiece *The Silver Darlings*.

The *Diamond* and Gunn's herring boats were sailing ships, but the
advent of steam meant a huge leap in the significance of ships and the sea
to Scotland. Much of the pioneering work was done by Scots in Scotland.
Patrick Miller of Dalswinton's experiment in 1788 with a steamboat on a
loch on his Dumfriesshire estate was followed by his steamboat experiments on the Forth and Clyde Canal in 1790. The same location saw
William Symington's trials of the paddle steamer *Charlotte Dundas* in 1801.
That none of these successful experiments resulted in the commercial

exploitation of the principle is attributable to a variety of reasons, such as Patrick Miller's dilettantism and Symington's bad luck in becoming embroiled in internal politics within the Forth and Clyde Canal Company. Symington was plagued with ill fortune; after his Forth and Clyde Canal work was stopped he was engaged by the Duke of Bridgewater, a great English canal promoter, to build steam tugs for his canals – sadly the Duke died in 1803, before Symington could start work, and the order was cancelled by Bridgewater's executors.

Scotland was also at the very heart of the development of the steam engine. James Watt from Greenock, working as a scientific instrument maker for Glasgow University, developed and patented the separate condenser for the steam engine, which made engines considerably more efficient – previously the cylinder had to be heated and cooled in each cycle, but the separate condenser allowed heat to be retained within the cylinder and the spent steam cooled separately. Watt himself was sceptical about high-pressure steam and indeed the application of steam to ships and is reported to have written to Henry Bell:

> How many noblemen, gentlemen and engineers have puzzled their brains and spent their thousands of pounds, and none of all these, nor yourself, have been able to bring the power of steam navigation to a successful issue.[4]

Nevertheless when the Watt & Boulton patent for the separate condenser expired in 1800, access to this technology was liberated in time for the first steamships to come into being.

The 19th-century Clyde saw a remarkable number of innovations and developments which became part of the world's shipping scene. The move from wood to iron and then to steel construction was nowhere more enthusiastically adopted than on the Clyde, and the development of Robert Napier's iron shipbuilding yard at Govan from 1841 was as significant a development as any other. Napier was not only a major force in Clyde shipbuilding with an order book that would include warships for Denmark, the Netherlands and Turkey, and merchant ships for most of the world, as well as significant contracts for the Royal Navy, such as HMS *Black Prince* (Chapter 8), but he earned the title of 'Father

---

[4] Morris, Edward, *The Life of Henry Bell*, Blackie & Sons, Glasgow, 1844

FIG. 1.3
Robert Napier
The father of Clyde Shipbuilding portrayed around the time
of his first Cunard contract.
Authors' Collection

of Clyde Shipbuilding' for the large number of other Clyde shipbuilders who trained under him or worked for him before going on to establish their own companies. Significant figures such as William Denny, John Elder and James and George Thomson had all passed through the Govan yard. In marine engineering the Clyde also pioneered change – the triple expansion engine, which made such a huge improvement to engine efficiency and ended the need for supplementary sail power in long-distance ships, was developed at Elder's yard by Alexander Kirk, yet another Napier apprentice.

With change and technical innovation came a growing reputation for quality. As we will see in considering the paddle steamer *Britannia* (Chapter 6), this reputation was earned at an early period. When Robert Napier was discussing with Samuel Cunard the plans for the first Cunarders, Napier wrote: 'I cannot and will not admit of anything being done or introduced into these engines but what I am satisfied with as sound and good.' Napier built his reputation on quality at any cost, even when this restricted his profits. When Napier died in 1879 an obituary notice said:

> He might have become a rich man much sooner than he did if he had scamped his work and had only pecuniary results in view. These he utterly disregarded. He was a poor financier but he was a noble workman, with a soul above money and meanness in all its forms.

Whether he was such a poor financier is questionable – he died a very rich man – but what is beyond question is that he considered his reputation at stake in every ship and engine he built and was prepared to sacrifice short-term gain for long-term benefit by his insistence on quality – from such attitudes the term 'Clydebuilt' took on the seal of quality that it was to enjoy for generations.

The Scottish marine engineer became a ubiquitous feature of the world's engine rooms. The Dumbarton writer and, incidentally, a former employee in Denny's yard, Tom Gallacher, quoted at the start of this chapter, could, writing in the mid 20th century, look at the passing ships on the Clyde and claim that 'their engine rooms were manned by OUR uncles and brothers and cousins'. Gallacher stood in a long tradition, touched on by Munro in the extract cited above, of literature crediting the canniest engineers to the Clyde. Nowhere is this more obvious than in Rudyard Kipling's remarkable 'McAndrew's Hymn', the reflections of a Scots chief engineer, a man formed equally by his Clydeside training and his Calvinist beliefs:

Lord, Thou hast made this world below the shadow of a dream,
An', taught by time, I tak' it so – excepting always Steam.
From coupler- flange to spindle-guide I see thy Hand, O God –
Predestination in the stride o' yon connectin'-rod.
John Calvin might ha' forged the same – enormous, certain, slow –
Ay, wrought it in the furnace-flame, *my* 'Institutio'.
I cannot get my sleep to-night, old bones are hard to please,
I'll stand the middle watch up here – alone with God an' these
My engines, after ninety days o' race an' rack an' strain
Through all the seas of all Thy world, slam-bangin' home again.
…
What I hae seen since ocean-steam began
Leaves me na doot for the machine: but what about the man?
The man that counts, wi' all his runs, one million miles of sea:
Four times the span from earth to moon… How far, O Lord, from Thee

McAndrew sees the passengers whom he has safely carried over the oceans leave the ship oblivious to his existence and role:

Then, at the last, we'll get to port an' hoist their baggage clear –
The passengers, wi' gloves and canes – an' this is what I'll hear:
'Well, thank you for a pleasant voyage. The tender's comin' now.'
While I go testin' follower-bolts and watch the skipper bow,
They've words for every one but me – shake hands wi' half the crew,
Except the dour Scots engineer, the man they never knew

McAndrew, 'the auld Fleet Engineer', has pride in his work, in his skills, in the performance of his engines and in his own integrity:

But I ha' lived an' I ha' worked. Be thanks to Thee, Most High!
An' I ha' done what I ha' done – judge Thou if ill or well.[5]

With this heritage it is little wonder that Scots, even those most tenuously connected with ships and the sea, feel some sort of 'special relationship'.

---

[5] Kipling, Rudyard, *Rudyard Kipling's Verse, inclusive edition, 1885–1932*, Hodder & Stoughton, London, 1933

This was observed back in 1861 when the *Black Prince* was launched. The reporter for the London *Times* wrote of the crowds who had turned out to see the launch on a wet February day:

> Among Londoners the launch of all the iron frigates ever built would not have drawn a thousand people together in such weather; but, strange to say, in Glasgow it appeared to make no manner of difference to the crowds that flocked to witness the ceremony.

He went on to speak of the sense of personal involvement with what was taking place. The launch of ships great and small continued to be major events on the Clyde and even long after their launch some ships can still attract crowds to the riverbank when they return to the waters of their birth. The QE2, when her cruise programme brings her to Greenock, is sure to attract huge numbers of spectators who line the roads for a view of the great liner and when the Royal Yacht *Britannia* (Chapter 17) came to the Clyde in 1997 on her last visit before she was decommissioned large crowds turned up for merely an exterior view – today she is, of course, a popular visitor attraction at Leith – sadly a berth on the river of her birth seemed to be unattainable.

One other dimension to Scotland's relationship to the sea not explicitly dealt with in any of the following chapters forms a sub-text to several and should perhaps be mentioned here – namely, Scotland and the Royal Navy.

The post-Union Navy is all too often thought of as an English service, which is perhaps unsurprising with the concentration of naval dockyards and harbours along the Channel coast and the high percentage of officers and men drawn from English coastal counties such as Hampshire, Dorset and Devon. However, the Scottish involvement in the post-Union Royal Navy was hugely significant. The period of the French wars of the late 18th and early 19th centuries, to look no further, demonstrates this. The critical battle of Camperdown in 1797 that neutralised the Dutch fleet was won by the Dundonian Adam Duncan. One of the prominent admirals of the period was George Keith Elphinstone, 1st Viscount Keith, born near Stirling, who commanded the Mediterranean and the Channel Fleets. The charismatic figure of Thomas Cochrane, whose single ship actions in the Mediterranean have been the inspiration of authors from Captain Marryat to Patrick O'Brian, was heir to the Scottish earldom of Dundonald.

If Scottish personnel have perhaps not had the attention that they

FIG. 1.4
Admiral Duncan
The victor of the Battle of Camperdown.
Authors' Collection

FIG. 1.5
Admiral Keith
One of the many distinguished Scottish admirals of the period.
Authors' Collection

might have had, then the role of Scotland as arsenal is certainly better documented, and *Black Prince, Hood* and *Vanguard* in this book stand as testimony to Scotland's contribution to the fleet. In the 20th century, as the threat from France declined and the rising power of Germany became more apparent, there was a repositioning of the Royal Navy from its traditional Channel bases to ports in Scotland, better suited to controlling the northern exits from the North Sea. The development of facilities at Rosyth, Invergordon and Scapa Flow, which became the principal bases for the Grand Fleet in the First World War reflect these new geo-political realities. The Clyde's position on the Atlantic, well removed from most threats, proved vital as a port in both world wars, as did such less-developed but highly valuable and heavily used harbours like Loch Ewe in Wester Ross, extensively used as a marshalling area for Russian convoys in the Second World War. In more recent years the deep water and easy access to the Atlantic offered by the Clyde's sea lochs has seen them become home to nuclear submarines, and today the United Kingdom's strategic nuclear deterrent is based in the Gareloch and a complex of facilities has been developed to support this presence.

The Scottish ships we have discussed in this book are, we feel, all significant and, to some extent, iconic, to use that convenient, if perhaps overused, adjective. There were many other ships and types of ships with strong claims to inclusion. The inclusion of the *Lusitania*, for example, obliged us to pass over the equally magnificent Clydebank Cunarder *Aquitania*, and the survival of the *Cutty Sark* ensured her inclusion at the expense of her rival, the great Aberdeen clipper *Thermopylae*.

Some ships which have strong Scottish connections have been omitted – perhaps most regrettably that remarkable maritime fossil HMS *Unicorn*, which, although launched at Chatham in 1824, has spent the past 133 years at Dundee and could be seen as Scottish by adoption. *Unicorn* (named, of course, after the heraldic supporter of the Scottish Royal Arms) is an almost totally unaltered frigate of the classic age. When built she was immediately laid up 'in ordinary' as part of the reserve fleet and then was used as a powder hulk before coming north to serve as a drill ship and floating headquarters. In consequence she avoided the many re-fits and alterations that would have been inevitable had she seen sea-going service with the Fleet and, as a result, today we have in Dundee perhaps the least-altered old wooden hull in good condition anywhere in the world.

FIG. 1.6
HMS *Unicorn*
The veteran frigate now preserved at Dundee.
VisitScotland Angus & Dundee

Many ships have had considerable relevance to Scottish history and one could make a case for including the ships of the ill-fated Darien Company, or even the French-built ships associated with the Jacobite risings – the *du Teillay*, which brought Charles Edward Stuart to Scotland, and *L'Herieux*, which took him back into exile; but choices had to be made and these, and the economically significant ships such as our fishing craft and oil industry ships, sadly had to be excluded.

A particular regret is that the great Scottish tradition of the racing yacht has had to be overlooked. In particular, Sir Thomas Lipton's gallant but unavailing attempt to build a yacht that would win back the America's Cup for Britain is a fascinating story of obsession and beautiful, elegant ships. It was also, largely because of Lipton's humble origins, a story that caught the public imagination in a way that other manifestations of this very rich man's sport had not. As Neil Munro's Glaswegian waiter and Kirk Beadle Erchie Macpherson observed in a story published in the *Glasgow Evening News* in June 1903, when *Shamrock III* was being readied for the contest:

> Shairly ye never read the papers. There's been naethin' in them a' this week past but Lipton's yats. Naebody needs to gang to the coast this summer; a' they need to dae's to bide at hame in bonny wee Gleska and spend their bawbees on newspapers.[6]

Indeed Erchie even meets Lipton at a function where he is on duty as a waiter and is told by the millionaire yachtsman:

> This sport's an awfu' harrassin' thing, the eyes o' the world's on me, and forbye, I ha'e to keep mind o' the names o' the sails and ropes and things, ye ha'e nae idea whit a job it is. Never you tak' to the yattin', Erchie.[7]

Shamrock III, designed by the famous Ayrshire yacht designers Fyfe, was built – in conditions of great secrecy in a covered building berth – by Denny of Dumbarton and was but one in a series of five great racing yachts that Lipton had built between 1899 and 1930 to contest the America's Cup – as Erchie suggested: 'A yat a year is Lipton's motto. He's fair hotchin' wi' yats; they're stickin' to his feet.'[8]

---

[6] Munro, Neil, *Erchie my droll friend*, Birlinn, Edinburgh, 2002
[7] Ibid
[8] Ibid

FIG 1.7
Shamrock III
One of Thomas Lipton's line of unsuccessful challengers for the America's Cup.
Authors' Collection

Sadly Lipton, despite his huge enthusiasm and equally huge investment, failed to win the coveted trophy. Indeed, a succession of British syndicates had attempted to win back the cup from the holders, the New York Yacht Club, but the Americans remained unbeaten for 25 challenges over 113 years, the longest winning streak in the history of sport. The 1958 challenger *Sceptre* and 1964 challenger *Sovereign* were both built by Alexander Robertson & Sons at Sandbank on the Firth of Clyde.

The great Scottish ship in the 21st century? Will there ever be new candidates for such a book? It is hard to be optimistic; the decline in Scottish shipbuilding with just one general commercial shipbuilder – Ferguson Shipbuilders at Port Glasgow on the lower Clyde – and the two BAE Systems yards engaged on naval work at Govan and Scotstoun on the upper Clyde, hardly represent grounds for optimism and there is no longer the capacity to build large ships. Despite the growth of air traffic the cargo market is still a booming one, UK marine freight traffic rose by two per cent in 2005 over 2004 to 586 million tons. This market is, however, largely being supplied by ships built elsewhere in the world. In 2004 there were 110 ships built in Scotland, with 5,400 workers engaged in the industry: at first glance this seems an encouragingly high output, however, 90 of these vessels were produced at 82 sites employing less than 25 people each, and would include small fishing vessels, pleasure craft, etc. Only 20 vessels came from 18 sites employing more than 25 employees – all in all a far cry from the great Clyde yards which previously counted their workforces in thousands.

This loss of capacity has meant that, for example, Cunard's contract for a new flagship, the *Queen Mary 2*, went to the French firm Chantiers de L'Atlantique at Saint-Nazaire, ending a tradition of over 150 years of Clyde-built Cunarders. The projected new aircraft carriers for the Royal Navy, at close on 300 metres length, will be too large to be built in any shipyard in the UK and will be built in modules, on the Clyde and elsewhere, and assembled in a dock, probably at Rosyth on the Firth of Forth.

There is perhaps little point in lamenting the loss of an industry which cannot now be recaptured but there is surely merit in celebrating a heritage and a history and in understanding where we once stood, and so we offer this look at Scotland's Great Ships to all who respond to the age-old allure of ships and the sea.

CHAPTER 2

Scotland's Earliest Ships

SPECULATION ABOUT the nature of ships used by Scots in earliest days is for the most part just that – speculation. However, inferences can be drawn from the archaeological record and the history of broad trends and developments in sea transport elsewhere in Western Europe, especially Scandinavia. In earliest days, two main Neolithic navigation routes can be assumed: firstly, the east coast or North Sea route that had probably led from the English Channel (or possibly a land-bridge from Europe); secondly, the short crossing from Western Scotland to Ireland, certainly, and perhaps Wales.

By the first millennium the Scots settling in what is approximately modern Argyll are supposed to have used varieties of skin boats or curraghs to make the crossing – peaceful trading, cultural missions or invasion routes are all suggested by the early records and other writings of the Irish and Welsh Celts, with different varieties of Celtic languages. The British or Welsh-speaking people of Strathclyde doubtless had seaborne links, just as the Irish Gaelic-speaking folk from Dalriada in Ireland would have seen the Irish Sea not as a barrier but as a springboard for invasion. Their new possessions in Scotland, also known as Dalriada, were to be the setting for the arrival of the civilizing force of the Celtic Church and Columba, its standard bearer, in the 6th century. Columba's crossing from Ireland and his subsequent ministry in the Hebrides and Western seaboard can be viewed as an important part of the Church's determination to use the maritime dimension to exert a pacifying influence upon the shadowy Pictish lands and to play a unifying role in the power politics of the emerging kingdoms. By the sixth century the land that we now call Scotland probably comprised the following emerging elements: the Scots of Dalriada; the Welsh-speaking inhabitants of Strathclyde; the 'problematic' Picts and the English-speaking people of the Lothian area.

What made the crossing from Ireland a practical consideration was the suitability of the western coasts of Scotland for the development of ships and boats, and especially the vessel known as the *curragh* in Irish

Gaelic. The deeply indented coastline of sea-lochs and kyles, together with many mountain ranges and deep forests, meant that travel by land was almost impossible – the corollary is that the possession of manageable sea-going vessels enabled first of all migration of peoples and, secondly, a capability for maintaining contact with their places of origin and scattered settlements. Some of these curraghs must have been a good size since it is probable that they were used to transport livestock and other bulky goods. By analogy with present day Inuit skin boats (and to some extent the reconstructed Irish-style St Brendan replica vessel planned and built by Tim Severin), it has been argued that they could have been up to 30 or 40 feet in length. Most historians accept that a crossing from Northern Ireland was feasible because of the favourable sailing conditions created by the flood tides that surge up the channels provided by Kilbrannan Sound, the Sound of Jura, the *Dorus Mor* off Crinan, and so on. Navigation was also likely to be assisted by the many prominent headlands and mountain peaks that were visible as landmarks, at least when weather conditions were good. The skin boats (made with a wooden framework and covered with ox hides) first appeared in Neolithic times and were probably developed and improved well into the first millennium AD. It was in just such a curragh that St Columba sailed from Loch Foyle to Iona, probably staging his voyage by making landings on Islay and Oronsay. Once embarked on his conversion of the Picts, Columba found ready to hand navigable waterways that would take him via the power centre of Dunadd, the Firth of Lorn and Loch Ness, to the heart of Pictland.

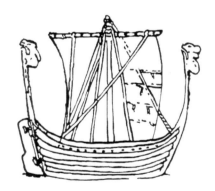

FIG. 2.1
Birlinn Drawing
The characteristic ship of the West Highlands in the medieval and early modern period. Image based on tomb at Rodel, Harris.
Comunn Birlinn

By then, another type of sailing vessel had also become a frequent sight in Scottish waters, especially in the west – the clinker-built boat or ship epitomised by the Norse or Viking longship with a number of particular Scottish variants, the best known of the latter being the birlinn. In time such clinker-built ships were to take wooden shipbuilding of a certain type to an absolute limit – the type where the longitudinal planking was, as it were, moulded into its overall shape or 'shell', rather than fixing the planks edge to edge to a framework or 'skeleton'. Again, it is only possible to make inferences from the substantial ship remains that have been found in Scandinavia, such as the Gokstad ship, that tell us almost all we know about perhaps the most iconic and awesome of all ships.

Predominant Ship Type on West Coast	Predominant Ship Type on East Coast
'SHELL TYPE'	'SKELETON TYPE'
• Strong central keel and stem and stern	• Framework built first to provide strong, rigid structure
• Usually clinker-built, i.e. over-lapping longitudinal flexible planking making a 'shell'	• Usually edge-to-edge longitudinal planking on top of 'skeleton'
• Examples: Scandinavian longship; birlinn; West Highland galley	• Examples: Western European 'carvel' type of ship such as James IV's *Michael*
• Size limited by structure	• Size not limited to same extent

At any rate, it was the dreaded longships with their crews of Vikings, ruled over by mighty sea-kings, which were, throughout much of the first millennium, operating in Scottish waters, most certainly in the Norse jarldom of Orkney but probably in the extensive Hebridean archipelago as well. This was culturally significant too, because it probably meant to some degree alien damage to the social and cultural bridge with Ireland, but fortunately not before (in a famous instance) Iona's monks were able to contrive the removal of the precious Book of Kells from Columba's island to the (relatively) safer monastery in County Meath in Ireland. Iona was ravaged by Vikings five times in all, leaving as part of a searing folk-memory the name of Martyrs' Bay, close to the pier. It is intriguing to speculate that, in one instance at any rate, the coracle-type vessel used by the Columban monks may have been capable of eluding the faster Norse

FIG. 2.2
Gokstad Ship
The magnificent vessel preserved in Oslo's Vikingskipshuset.
Seth White

raiders, and saved the 'Chief Relic of the Western World' for civilization. More often, however, there was slaughter and destruction. Apart from the slender evidence of the Scandinavian ship remains, the sagas provide our best indications of interaction of an unfavourable kind between Gaels and Norsemen:

> Fire played in the (trees) of Lewis; it mounted up to heaven. Far and wide the people were driven to flight. The fire gushed out of their houses... The glad wolf reddened tooth and claw in many a mortal wound within Tiree... the people of Mull ran to exhaustion. Greenland's king caused maids to weep south in the islands.
>
> *The Magnus Saga*[1]

By the 12th century, the Scots and Gaels were in a position to challenge 'the fury of the Norsemen'. Their response was led by a new player in the game, who boasted a Scoto-Norse ancestry, and his name was Somerled, which means 'Summer Traveller', an allusion to the Vikings' habit of voyaging (and plundering) in summer. The Norse ships that Somerled found himself facing as King of Argyll had been for 300 years completely invincible. They were longer, stronger and swifter – they also carried more fighting men and spare crews so that they could operate far from bases in Man and Orkney or further afield. Somerled's galleys or birlinns (from the Gaelic – *short blade*) were transformed or replaced by a new breed of ship that could confront the longships. From the evidence of an image on Somerled's Seal – given on a charter to Paisley Abbey by his son Ragnald – Somerled's new ships, his secret weapons, seem to have incorporated two innovations – a fighting mast-top that could command the decks if the Vikings boarded, and a new type of hinged steering rudder that gave the Islesmen the benefits of quicker turning and manoeuvrability. In 1156, the chronicles tell us, Somerled's new fleet defeated a Norse battle fleet off the west coast of Islay in the Battle of the Epiphany, probably the only such defeat at sea in Norse history.

From then on Somerled made Islay his base and the dynasty was founded that would lead to the Lordship of the Isles – at its peak the bearers of the name held sway over land and sea from Assynt to the Mull

---

[1] *The Magnus or Orkneyinga Saga* quoted in Murray, W. H., *Islands of Western Scotland*, Eyre Methuen, London, 1973

of Kintyre and from Lochaber to Rockall. Treaties were sometimes made with Norwegian kings and other Vikings, not surprising when it is realised that the seat of power of the Kings of Scots was less accessible, in more ways than one, than Norway by sea. However, having led a fleet of 150 ships into the Firth of Clyde in 1164, Somerled himself was killed at Renfrew, far from his base; thereafter the Scots monarchy and the Lordship of the Isles were again at arm's length. Similarly, in 1263, the Norwegians under Hakon (their battle fleet blown on to the Largs shore) were defeated by the forces of the shrewd Alexander III. Although the Islesmen contributed a substantial force to Bruce at Bannockburn, hostility continued to grow between the Kings of Scots and the Highlands and Islands.

Petty quarrels and wars among the clans became a regular feature of the Atlantic seaboard; as late as the '45 Rebellion fighting ships, still known as birlinns, were an important weapon available for Highland and Hebridean chieftains; we know this because of the survival of the marvellous epic poem, 'The Birlinn of Clanranald' by Alasdair MacMhaighstir Alasdair (Captain Alasdair Macdonald). These verses were composed by a schoolmaster turned soldier, and they give a graphic account of the essential features of a type of vessel that remained essentially unchanged from the time of Somerled 600 years previously. Partly, they are about vaunting the prestige of the clan chief in time of war, partly they are about the efficiency, the fitness for purpose of the product, of the shipwright's skills. Clanranald's sailors pray for a blessing on the new birlinn:

> Our mast-hoops and yards do thou bless,
> Our masts and our ropes one and all,
> Our stays and our haulyards preserve,
> And let no mischance befall.
> The Holy Ghost be at the helm,
> Show the right track to go,
> He knoweth each port 'neath the sun,
> On His care ourselves we throw.[2]

The necessity for skilful navigation, or keeping to the 'right track', is seen in the verses calling for a look-out man in the ship's bows:

---

[2] Alasdair MacMhaighstir Alasdair, Captain Alasdair Macdonald, *The Birlinn of Clanranald* quoted in *Echoes of the Sea*, Canongate, Edinburgh, 1998

Let an ocean cloud-seer rise and stand
At the bow,
And let him sure knowledge give us
Of our harbour,
Let him look to the four quarters
Of the heavens,
And let him tell the steersman,
'Right she goeth';
Let him catch and note the landmarks
With keen vision,
Since they and the God of weather
Are our lode-star.

So the finding of landmarks was still a principal method of coastal navigation as late as the 18th century. However, the armaments carried by this war galley on a voyage to Carrickfergus in Ulster were a mixture of old and new:

God's blessing be upon our swords,
Our keen grey brands of Spain,
Our heavy coats of mail, on which
The sword-sweep falls in vain.

Our gauntlets and our corselets,
Our deftly-figured shields,
Whate'er our belts do carry,
Whatever warrior wields.

Our polished bows of yew-tree,
That bend in battle's din,
Our birchen shafts that split not,
Cased in grim badger's skin.

Bless Thou our dirks and pistols,
Our good kilts in their folds,
And every kind of warlike gear
McDonell's bark now holds!

Meanwhile, the other North European tradition of shipbuilding had developed along separate lines, mainly on the eastern coastline. The capacious yet sophisticated sailing vessels that owed little to the galley or longship tradition were prominent in the trading links that Scotland began to develop with the Low Countries. From this tradition was to emerge an individual ship that, in its brief career, became celebrated at home and abroad. This great ship, the *Michael*, was to be seen as a fitting symbol of the glamorous and dramatic reign and international aspirations of its royal progenitor.

CHAPTER 3

Great Michael (1507–1521)

THE SCOTTISH TRADITION of shipbuilding developed with two main strands: one the Norse tradition of shipbuilding, descended from the Viking long-ship via the birlinn or West Highland galley, and the second reflecting the mainstream European tradition which was associated with, in particular, the Spanish and Portuguese sailing vessels. It was the latter tradition that influenced Scotland's earliest identifiable sailing vessel, the early 16th-century ship usually referred to as the *Great Michael*, although the evidence suggests that contemporaries knew her simply as the *Michael*. The most frequently used technical name for the *Michael* is a carrack, as mentioned by Chaucer in *The Summoner's Tale*, and in the *Oxford English Dictionary* as: 'a large ship of burden, also fitted for warfare, such as those... used by the Portuguese in trading with the East Indies.' Whatever her exact description – and any details of her specification are extremely hazy – we know that the *Michael* was very much a personal project of Scotland's very own Renaissance prince, King James IV (1473–1513), who ordered the laying of her keel on the sands of Newhaven (the 'new harbour'), near to Leith, 500 years ago in the year 1507. Several contemporary reports bore witness that the *Michael* was an object of wonder and awe to all who saw her – truly iconic. The rest-lessly energetic young king's motive for building her was partly military, partly in search of personal and political prestige. He hoped to create a navy that would be capable of protecting Scotland's coastline and ship-ping routes, especially against his southern neighbour, and capable of increasing the realm of Scotland's standing in 16th-century Europe. James seems to have been, more than most, alert to what has been called the technological advantage of such 'large and capacious ships' and that by building such ships monarchs like himself – and other emerging Western European nation states in the 15th and 16th centuries – had to hand an important instrument of economic and territorial power.

To this end he had chosen his ground well by taking some shrewd strategic decisions. Since a sandbar at Leith effectively placed limits on the size of ships that could be built at the usual naval dockyards in that port, James acquired a stretch of the Forth coastline one mile west of Leith at the bay called the 'new haven' – a natural harbour, with deep water, on whose shingle beach the new navy (or at least the *Michael*) could be built. Craftsmen came from Flanders, Scandinavia, Spain and Portugal. France also contributed skilled artisans and wrights, and in due course James felt able to write boastingly to his French fellow-monarch Louis XII: 'We have been building of a fleet and we labour at it with great zeal.' James used some exaggeration in describing his building programme as amounting to the creation of a fleet – since no other Scottish vessel then or for many years afterwards could approach the *Michael*'s magnitude. One of the adornments of James's court, William Dunbar, the greatest of the makars (poets), wrote a poem for James, 'Sir, you have many Worthy Servants'. This draws a brief yet vivid picture of the kind of busy scene that could have been witnessed at the naval yards of Leith or more especially the harbour at Newhaven. The 'ballingars' that Dunbar refers to are, however, small ships, quite dwarfed by the magnificent product of a vast technological advance that the *Michael* represented:

> … carvers and carpenters,
> Builders of barks and ballingars,
> Masons lying upon the land,
> And shipwrights hewing upon the strand.[1]

There is a curious echo of this last line in the old ballad 'Sir Patrick Spens', in which the eponymous ill-fated Scottish sea-captain is depicted as 'walking on the strand'. We can deduce that this 'strand' is somewhere on the Forth's Fife shore near to where the king sits 'in Dunfermline toon'. This is before Sir Patrick learns the dreaded news that he (as 'a skeely skipper') must reluctantly accept the captaincy of the king's 'new ship', and follow orders 'at this time of year / to sail upon the sea!' That Spens's ship was, we might suppose, in the Northern European fashion of shipbuilding, can be deduced from the fact that she 'hoysed her sails on Monenday morn' rather than having oars used by a galley type of vessel.

---

[1] Dunbar, William, *The Poems of William Dunbar*, Canongate Classics, Edinburgh, 1999

The *Michael* was laid down in 1507 but was not completed until 1512, almost certainly an indication of the size and complexity of this, the greatest of warships of her day. A courtier's account gave a little more detail:

> The keel was laid of a ship that was to be the biggest that any had seen sail on the ocean.

The long build-time is more evidence to add to the best-known report of the *Michael's* impressive size and scale, and of her demands on resources and building materials; the report comes from the *Historie and Cronicles of Scotland* by Robert Lindsay of Pitscottie. Lindsay was an otherwise obscure Fife laird who compiled a chronicle of events in Scotland, extending from the 1430s (the period of James II) to his own time (the 1570s). Lindsay draws upon earlier histories as well as his own direct experience and others' accounts – in the following extract he makes use of something quite like modern interview techniques:

> ... the King built a great ship [*note the placing of the Renaissance prince at the very centre of the project*] called the *Michael* which was a very monstrous great ship; for this ship took so much timber that she wasted all the woods in Fife, except Falkland wood, besides the timber that came out of Norway... The ship was twelve score feet in length, thirty-six feet within the walls, she was ten foot thick within the walls of oak planks, so that no cannon could do at her; she troubled all Scotland to get her ready for the sea and when she was committed to the sea, and under sail, she had cost the King £40,000 besides the ordnance and cannons that she bore. She had three hundred mariners to sail her, six score gunners to use her artillery, and a thousand men of war, besides captains, skippers and quartermasters... my informant was Captain Andrew Wood, principal captain of her, and Robert Barton, who was master skipper.[2]

It is thought that the *Michael* (named after the Archangel) may have been Europe's first 1,000-ton vessel, twice the size of Henry VIII's ship *Mary Rose*; with four masts and very heavily armed with 24 main guns

---

[2] Lindsay Robert, of Pitscottie: from *Historie and Cronicles of Scotland*, quoted in Osborne, Brian D & Armstrong, Ronald, *Echoes of the Sea, Scotland and the Sea, an anthology*, Canongate, Edinburgh, 1998

(probably firing stone balls) on the broadside, together with lesser guns and a basilisk pointing forward, with two others astern. A basilisk was a large brass cannon capable of throwing a shot of some 200 pounds, and is further evidence that warships of this period were designed as floating artillery platforms more than anything else. There is a story, probably apocryphal, that on occasions James's great ship was armed with the huge cannon Mons Meg that is still to be seen at Edinburgh Castle, but certainly a good part of her firepower was distributed so as to be able to concentrate fire at close quarters even on her own decks. This was because the tactics likely to be employed by her skipper were to 'grapple' with the enemy and thereafter rely on this firepower and her superior capacity for carrying armed men to be deployed in hand-to-hand fighting. Features such as these were essential parts of the desirable specification for a state-of-the-art warship. More than previous ships built in the British Isles, the *Michael* was designed from the first to carry heavy artillery, all (apart from the somewhat unlikely case of Mons Meg) specially cast for the ship by Robert Borthwick, the king's 'Master Melter' (or iron smelter) at Edinburgh Castle.

Immediately after James's triumphant parading of the *Michael*, other monarchs joined in what seems to have been a naval arms race: in the last year of James IV's reign he was spending around one fifth of his annual income on paying the crew of the *Michael*. James's ally, Louis of France, eventually purchased the *Michael* from Scotland after James's death at Flodden in 1513. James's adversary, Henry VIII, responded to the appearance of the *Michael* by rapidly ordering the construction of the ship known as the *Great Harry*, another 1,000-ton monster. From then on the sequence of technological rivalry, leading to progress in shipbuilding, can be traced right down to the emergence in the 17th century of the English 'ships of the line'. It would be interesting to speculate how important the influence of the 'Old Scots Navy' was, as represented by the *Michael*, upon the Royal Navy of Drake and Blake.

It has been argued that James IV – very conscious of his standing in 16th-century Christendom – envisaged his new ship as something grander and more significant than simply a challenge to the Auld Enemy; it has even been conjectured that he saw her as an essential and formidable component of a new post-medieval crusade of European monarchies ranged against the power of the vast Islamic Ottoman Empire. However,

FIG. 3.1
James IV
The Royal inspiration behind the *Michael.*
Authors' Collection

there had to be considerable revision of this dream when the more familiar demands of the Auld Alliance re-asserted themselves and James was called upon by France to do what had been asked of many a king of Scots before him – to invade England as a diversionary tactic. Accompanying this invasion, a naval strike force was assembled to attack English possessions in France, but in the event the group of ships led by the *Michael* only saw some sparse action at Carrickfergus in Ireland at the same time as the catastrophe that overcame James's land forces (and the king himself) at Flodden in Northumberland in September 1513. Soon afterwards the hugely expensive and largely redundant *Michael* was leased to the French directly and she was sold to Louis XII by order of the Lords of Council in April 1514:

> The Lords ratify the selling of the King's great ship with tackle and apparel for 40,000 livres to the French King. Done for the public weal and profit of the realm.

Certainly, while in French ownership, the *Michael* led the blockading squadron that captured the Spanish port of Fuentarrabia in October 1521; however, no further significant action was seen by the *Michael* and she disappears from history. So ended the last occasion when a Scottish vessel, or arguably the Scots nation, could assume a comparable role with the first-rank powers of Europe.

CHAPTER 4

Emigrant Ships

IN OCTOBER 1773 James Boswell and Dr Samuel Johnson were touring the Highlands and the Hebrides and had reached Skye. Boswell records in his *Journal of a Tour to the Hebrides*:

> We performed, with much activity, a dance which, I suppose, the emigration from Skye has occasioned. They call it *America*. Each of the couples, after the common *involutions* and *evolutions,* successively whirls round in a circle, till all are in motion; and the dance seems intended to shew how emigration catches, till a whole neighbourhood is set afloat – Mrs McKinnon told me, that last year when a ship sailed from Portree for America, the people on shore were almost distracted when they saw their relatives go off; they lay down on the ground, tumbled, and tore the grass with their teeth. This year there was not a tear shed. The people on shore seemed to think that they would soon follow. This indifference is a mortal sign for the country.[1]

During the travellers' two months in the Highlands and Islands the topic of emigration came up repeatedly and at least two emigrant ships were encountered; the *Margaret of Clyde* and the *Nestor*, which Boswell inspected as she lay in Portree harbour:

> She was a very pretty vessel, and, as we were told, the largest in Clyde. Mr Harrison, the captain, shewed her to us. The cabin was commodious, and even elegant. There was a little library, finely bound.[2]

Evidently the *Nestor* was a cut above the average run of migrant ships.

There had always, of course, been emigration from Scotland, but it was usually small-scale and often not with the intention of permanent settlement. Scots had for centuries gone off to earn a living in Scandinavia, in the Baltic states, to serve in the armies of more or less anyone who

---

[1] Boswell, James, *Journal of a tour to the Hebrides*, Oxford University Press, London, 1930

[2] Ibid

would hire them, to study law or medicine in France or the Netherlands. In many cases they intended to return to Scotland having gained what they wanted from the foreign land, although, of course, many never returned and settled down happily in their new land. The Russian poet Lermontov and the Norwegian composer Grieg are just two descendants of such Scottish migrants.

Mass migration from Scotland, however, was very much a phenomenon which developed in the second half of the 18th century. A detailed account of its causes are beyond the scope of this chapter, but the social and economic changes in the Highlands after the collapse of the Jacobite risings of 1715 and 1745 are at the root of the movement. In the old system in the Highlands clan chiefs had measured their importance by the length of their rent-roll and the number of fighting men they could muster and would have discountenanced any movement to depopulate their areas, particularly if that depopulation would involve the young men and women of the community. The ending of the military role of the clans; the move to other forms of agriculture, particularly the conversion of large areas of the Highlands to sheep farms which could be run by a small, often Lowland, workforce; and the increasing commercialisation of relationships between landowner and tenant all meant that there were many pressures to remove the population from these areas. This was not just the movement of young and ambitious people seeking fortune overseas, but the removal, more or less unwillingly, of whole communities. Dr Johnson talked to a farmer in Inverness-shire and set his views down in his *Journey to the Western Islands*:

> From him we first heard of the general dissatisfaction, which is now driving the Highlanders into the other hemisphere; and when I asked him whether they would stay at home, if they were well treated, he answered with indignation, that no man willingly left his native country. Of the farm, which he himself occupied, the rent had, in twenty-five years, been advanced from five to twenty pounds, which he found himself so little able to pay, that he would be glad to try his fortunes in some other place.[3]

One estimate puts the number of Scots who emigrated to North America

---

[3] Johnson, Samuel, *Journey to the Western Isles*, Oxford University Press, London, 1930

and the West Indies in the period 1763–75 at around 25,000 – a total which grew in the 19th century and which was facilitated by the improvements in shipping. Between 1825 and 1938, 2.3 million people left Scotland for overseas destinations. Although this number is subject to qualification, because of under-recording in some periods and also because substantial numbers of migrants found that the grass was not actually greener on the other shore and returned to Scotland, it can be taken as a broadly accurate approximation of the loss the country sustained in just over a century.

The implications of this outflow of population are considerable and included the development of a major shipping industry in Scotland to service this trade. We shall look at some 19th- and 20th-century examples of the ships that served this trade rather than attempt to catalogue all the many hundreds of vessels that carried Scots overseas. One particular early example must be included simply because of its iconic nature.

In the early period the emigrant trade was carried out very largely by ships that were well below the standard of the *Nestor* that James Boswell had admired in Portree harbour and which were not built primarily as passenger transporters. There was a substantial trade in timber from North America to Britain and ships carrying timber eastwards needed a return cargo, and emigrants proved to be a useful and profitable cargo. The quality of many of these early emigrant ships left much to be desired and conditions on the long passages were often appalling.

In July 1773 the ship *Hector* left Loch Broom for Pictou, Nova Scotia for what turned out to be a 12 week crossing. The *Hector* was so rotten that the passengers could pick the wood out of her hull with their fingers, food ran short, disease was rampant, 18 children died of small-pox or dysentery and the 200 passengers eventually reached land on 15 September, to face the challenges of a Canadian winter and a new life in totally alien surroundings.

The migrant experience was well summed up in the 'Canadian Boat Song' published anonymously in *Blackwood's Magazine* in 1829. The authorship is sometimes attributed to the novelist John Galt, who had considerable experience of colonial life, being an agent for emigration in Upper Canada and who founded the town of Guelph, in what is now Ontario.

From the lone shieling of the misty island,
Mountains divide us, and the waste of seas –
Yet still the blood is strong, the heart is Highland,
And we in dreams behold the Hebrides!
Fair these broad meads, these hoary woods are grand;
But we are exiles from our fathers' land.[4]

Nor was North America the only destination for Scots migrants. From the mid 19th century Australia and New Zealand attracted many Scots and the development of the South Island of New Zealand owes much to organised settlement by Scots in areas such as Otago and Dunedin. Scottish shipping lines, such as the Albion Line whose clippers like the *Peter Denny* or the *City of Dunedin* traded to New Zealand, carried many Scots settlers to the far side of the world. These voyages were considerably better regulated and safer than the early migrant traffic to North America. In March 1863 Patrick Henderson & Co. – the predecessor of the Albion Line – could advertise the sailing of the *City of Dunedin* under the supervision of an emigration officer who ensured that stores were adequate and the steerage accommodation, the cheapest and most basic way to travel, was properly equipped. The *City of Dunedin,* a 195 foot long, 1070 ton register ship newly built at Dumbarton by Denny & Rankin, also offered the presence on board of a surgeon and a teacher. Many families made the trip out to New Zealand and as passages could be of 80 or 90 days' duration it was felt important that children's education should not be neglected; it was a Scottish shipping line after all. The more affluent migrant could travel in cabins on the poop deck of the ship, in, as the advertisement said, 'state rooms of unusual size', and with access to plunge and shower baths. A passage from the Clyde to Otago in such accommodation cost £30.

Ships such as the *City of Dunedin's* consort the *Robert Henderson* carried migrants on assisted passages funded by the colonial authorities and sailed under contract with the authorities and carried a surgeon and a matron on board. On these extremely long voyages to Australasia, the age of the pure sailing ship lasted much longer than on the North Atlantic routes. The simple matter of geography, combined with the relative

---

[4] Galt, John (attrib.) quoted in MacQueen, John & Scott, Tom, *The Oxford Book of Scottish Verse*, Oxford University Press, Oxford, 1966

inefficiency of the marine engines of the period, meant that ships could not carry coal sufficient for the passage, nor were there convenient coaling stations along most of the way, the long passage of the Southern Ocean, for example, offering no prospect of refuelling. However, the swift clippers of the Albion Line could record quick, and more importantly, safe passages. The *James Nicol Fleming,* built in 1869 at Port Glasgow by Robert Duncan, made a record passage in 1873 of 73 days from the Clyde to Otago, carrying 280 passengers, mostly assisted immigrants, including 58 single females. There was, in the early days of migration to New Zealand, a marked gender imbalance in the colony, and young women who would work as domestic servants were in great demand.

In August 1879, the Glasgow-based Anchor Line steamer *Devonia* sailed from the Clyde for New York with a mixed bag of emigrants:

> There were Scots and Irish in plenty, a few English, a few Americans, a good handful of Scandinavians, a German or two, and one Russian; all now belonging for ten days to one small iron country on the deep.[5]

So wrote one of the passengers, the novelist Robert Louis Stevenson, travelling to the United States to be reunited with Fanny Osbourne, the married American woman he had fallen in love with in France. Stevenson, although anxious to see the reality of emigrant life, travelled in the superior second cabin:

> I had some work to finish on the voyage, and was advised to go by the second cabin, where at least I should have a table at command.[6]

Stevenson notes, in *The Amateur Emigrant,* that the steerage fare was six guineas and he had paid eight guineas for second cabin. However, as the steerage passenger had to provide his own bedding and dishes, and as the diet in second cabin was slightly more varied and of better quality, Stevenson concluded that the difference in price was almost nominal. There was also the question of social class: 'In the steerage there are males and females, in the second cabin, ladies and gentlemen.'

The *Devonia* had been built in 1877 at Barrow and was a 4,270 gross tonnage ship of 400 feet length and was scheduled to perform the

---

[5] Stevenson, Robert Louis, *From Scotland to Silverado*, Belknap Press, Cambridge, Mass., 1966

[6] Ibid

crossing from the Clyde to New York, via Moville, Lough Foyle, in nine and a half days. She would be employed on this route until 1893 and was eventually scrapped at Hamburg in 1899.

The Anchor Line had been carrying passengers between the Clyde and North America from the 1850s and the emigrant trade formed a large part of its business. At the start of the 20th century they invested heavily in new and larger ships for the Glasgow to New York route with the *Columbia* of 1902 to be followed by the *Caledonia* (1904), *California* (1907) and *Cameronia* (1911) setting new standards for the route.

When *Columbia*, the first of these '4 Cs', was launched from the Partick yard of D&W Henderson in 1902, this steel twin-screw vessel was hailed as 'the largest and finest vessel ever built for the Glasgow and New York route'. *Columbia*, unlike rival companies' ships which sailed from Greenock, departed from the Anchor Line's own terminal at Yorkhill Quay close to the heart of the city, and she swiftly established a special place in the affections of Clyde people. As a Glasgow magazine wrote in 1905 when *Columbia's* first skipper, Captain Walter Baxter, was promoted to command of the new *Caledonia*:

> Every four weeks the fine lines and three raking funnels of the *Columbia*, funnels which distinguish her from all the other steamers trading from the Clyde, may be seen passing along the Firth on Sunday morning, or at the beginning of the outward voyage on the following Saturday, and at many watering places on the Clyde her appearance is eagerly awaited by the visitors.

Just as in the days of the *Devonia*, the Anchor Line ships made a call at Moville in Lough Foyle for the Irish trade. Scottish and Irish migrants were not the only occupants of the third class or steerage accommodation favoured by the emigrants. The Glasgow to New York route was favoured by many European migrants and the passenger lists for *Columbia's* first crossing in May 1902 shows that the steerage accommodation, which could house 750 passengers, was a temporary home to large numbers of Norwegians and Swedes, Danes and Finns, Polish Jews, Russians, Romanians and Austrians. Clearly there was a significant trade between European ports and Scotland, feeding these migrants into the Anchor Line route.

The 8,292 gross ton *Columbia* could also accommodate around 200 first class and 400 second class passengers, in considerably more comfort than the third class or steerage passengers. However, times had moved on since Stevenson's experience on the *Devonia*. Describing the new ship, the *Glasgow Herald* wrote:

> It must not be forgotten, also, that for this class the owners now provide bed and bedding, white tablecloths, and eating utensils of every kind.

A sitting room for women and children and a smoking room for men were also provided in third class.

The passengers on *Columbia* and her sister ships were not, of course, all migrants, but the vast majority of third class passengers and a good number of those travelling in first or second class were leaving their homelands forever. The Anchor Line provided one ship per week from Glasgow to New York, and although they would not necessarily be running at full capacity, this one line alone could move around 1,300 passengers a week from Scotland and Ireland to the United States, and in the years before the First World War the Anchor Line was only one of a number of companies sailing from the Clyde to North America. The Donaldson Line, serving Montreal, or the Allan Line, connecting the Clyde with Montreal, Quebec and Boston, offered alternative services.

Columbia would continue on the Atlantic crossing, with a break for war service as the armed merchant cruiser HMS *Columbella*, until 1925 and completed 208 round trips between Glasgow and New York and carried a total of 165,789 passengers. A short second career followed under the Greek flag before she was broken up at Venice in 1929.

It was hardly surprising that the migrant trade attracted many companies to Scotland. Canadian Pacific Railways had the emigrant ship *Metagama* built at Barclay Curle's yard in 1914 and placed her initially on the Liverpool to St John's route in 1915. After war service as a troop transport, she resumed sailings and served the company's Glasgow to Canada route. Canadian Pacific was a major force in the Atlantic with around 30 ships engaged in the trade in 1914.

The *Metagama* has a particular place in the folklore of emigration largely due to her April 1923 sailing. In a procedure reminiscent of the era of Boswell and Johnson she made a special call at Stornoway in Lewis and there took on board 400 young men and 20 women who were emigrating

FIG. 4.1
Columbia
The Anchor Line ship traded between Scotland, Ireland and New York carrying many emigrants.

Authors' Collection

FIG. 4.2
Metagama
The Canadian Pacific ship noted for its role in emigration
from the Western Isles.
Authors' Collection

to Canada. This large number, huge in the context of a thinly populated rural area, made headline news throughout the United Kingdom. A collection earlier that month from the southern Hebrides by the same company's *Marloch* had not attracted quite the same level of coverage. *The Times* noted that most of the emigrants were crofters and fishermen, nearly all single men, who were going out to work on Canadian farms. The majority of emigrants were ex-servicemen who were unemployed due to the decline in the fishing industry or shortage of crofting tenancies.

As *Metagama* lay off Stornoway and the emigrants, average age 22, were ferried out, the provost and councillors of Stornoway were entertained to lunch on board. On the luncheon table was a large bouquet of flowers sent by Lord Leverhulme, who had completed his purchase of Lewis and Harris in 1919 and whose plans for its economic revival had been frustrated. His wishes for a good voyage were echoed in a telegram from the local MP who wished the emigrants well in their new lives. The Minister of Stornoway United Presbyterian Church handed over a Gaelic Bible to each emigrant. *The Times* concluded its report by noting that during the weekend nearly 5,000 emigrants left the Clyde in four vessels, including the *Metagama,* which had called at Glasgow to collect more migrants before sailing for Canada. The *Metagama,* 12,420 tons displacement, 520 feet overall, could accommodate 516 passengers in cabin class and 1,138 in third class. By the 1920s most companies in the emigrant trade had simplified the traditional three-class structure to two classes, Cabin and Third – the *Columbia,* for example, had been converted to a two-class ship in 1922. The *Metagama* even came equipped with a children's nursery.

The *Metagama* was to have a somewhat chequered career. On her next crossing from Glasgow she collided in the Clyde off Dumbarton with the Hogarth Line's cargo vessel *Baron Vernon.* A year later she was stranded off Newfoundland following a collision. In 1927 she was transferred to the Canadian Pacific's Antwerp to Montreal route. With the coming of the Depression emigrant traffic declined and she was scrapped in 1934.

In later years the famous *Empress* liners of Canadian Pacific would continue the trade between the Clyde and Canada, carrying business and holidaymakers, emigrants and former emigrants coming back to visit the land of their origins. After the Second World War, Canadian Pacific resumed services from the Clyde with the *Empress of Scotland* (ex *Empress of Japan*) – a product of the Fairfield shipyard in 1929. She sailed from Liverpool and called at Greenock to uplift passengers who were ferried out to her as she lay at the Tail of the Bank. The Canadian Pacific liners continued the tradition of Clyde to Canada sailings into the late 1960s, eventually with two liners, *Empress of Canada* and *Empress of England*, providing services between April and November – cruising in warmer waters occupied these ships in the stormy winter months. The *Empress* fleet and the Clyde/Canada trade declined in the face of competition from jet aircraft and in November 1971 the last Canadian Pacific liner, *Empress of Canada*, docked at Liverpool, ending 68 years of Atlantic service.

CHAPTER 5

PS *Comet* (1812–20)

THE PADDLE STEAMER *Comet* is, in many ways, the least impressive of all the great Scottish ships discussed in this book. Small, a mere 42 feet in length as originally built; underpowered, fitted at first with a 3 horsepower engine; and with a crew of just four, she may at first sight seem an ill-matched companion to the great liners like the *Lusitania,* or warships like the *Michael* or HMS *Hood.* Yet the story of Scottish dominance in shipbuilding and marine engineering, a dominance that lasted from the mid 19th to the early 20th century, undoubtedly has its roots in this little wooden ship.

In 1812 steamboats were not really a complete novelty; the English inventor Jonathan Hulls had patented a steamboat as early as 1736, the French Marquis D'Abbans had, in 1783, demonstrated a steamship on the River Saone; in Scotland the experiments on loch and canal of Patrick Miller of Dalswinton in 1788 and 1790 had been successful and William Symington's work on the canal steamer *Charlotte Dundas* between 1800 and 1802 had only been stopped because of internal politics within the Forth and Clyde Canal Company. In the United States, Robert Fulton had successfully introduced a steamship onto the North River in New York State in 1807.

However, in 1812 nobody in Europe had yet managed to build and operate a commercial steamship and nowhere had one been built which was capable of operating in open waters. This was the claim to fame of Henry Bell, builder and owner of the *Comet.* Bell was hardly the inventor or the engineer of this pioneering steamship – the hull was constructed by John Wood at Port Glasgow, the engine was a land engine built by John Robertson, and the boiler was constructed to Bell's order by David Napier. Bell's role was that of visionary, entrepreneur and coordinator. On 11 August 1812 the Glasgow papers carried his advertisement announcing the commencement of services between Glasgow, Greenock and Helensburgh by the steam packet boat *Comet,* designed to sail by 'the power of Wind, Air and Steam'. When the *Glasgow Herald* of 10 August had reported the arrival, at the city's Broomielaw harbour, of 'a beautiful and commodious

Steam boat on the Clyde. near Dumbarton.

FIG. A

Steamboat on the Clyde.

A lithograph from William Daniell's *A Voyage Around Great Britain*. The picture, done in 1817, just five years after the *Comet's* first voyage, depicts one of the first generation of Clyde steamers off Dumbarton.

Authors' Collection

FIG. B

Aquitania

An early postcard of the classic four-funnelled Cunard liner in New York
harbour. *Aquitania* was built at Clydebank in 1913 and went into service
in May 1914. She was slower than the *Lusitania* but was renowned as the 'ship
beautiful'. After a long career she was broken up at Faslane on the Gareloch in 1950.

Authors' Collection

FIG. C

Hector

A full scale replica of the Dutch-built emigrant ship that took 200 Highland migrants from Loch Broom to Nova Scotia in 1773. She forms the centrepiece of the Hector Heritage Quay in Pictou, Nova Scotia.

Pictou Antigonish Regional Library

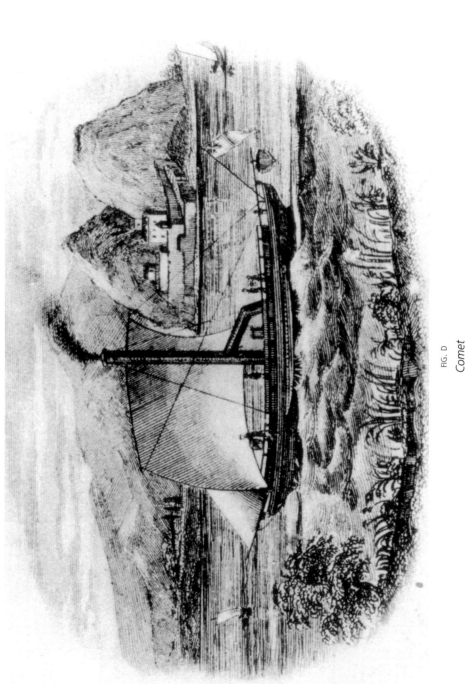

FIG. D

Comet

Henry Bell's advertisement for the *Comet* promised that it would sail by the power of wind, air and steam and this illustration shows the large square sail rigged on the funnel. It is interesting to compare the funnel in this illustration with that in 5.1.

FIG. E

Britannia

The first Cunarder into service, the paddle steamer *Britannia* as depicted by the noted American marine artist Samuel Ward Stanton (1870–1912). Stanton was a passenger on the maiden voyage of the *Titanic* in 1912. He boarded her at Cherbourg and was drowned when she sank.

Mariners Museum, Newport News, Virginia

FIG. F

Black Prince & Warrior

A late 19th century painting of Britain's first two iron-clad ships by Charles Nixon. The two ships were from the same design but for

FIG. G

Cutty Sark

Alone of the classic Scottish clippers *Cutty Sark* has been saved and now sits at Greenwich – a setting remote from her birthplace on the Leven and the wool quays of Australia but one of undoubted grandeur and relevance.

Cutty Sark Trust

FIG. H

Glenlee
After a long and varied career the *Glenlee* has returned to the river
of her birth and to a secure future in the care of the Clyde Maritime Trust. This view
shows her in her current berth at Yorkhill Quay.
Jim Ramsay

FIG. 5.1
Comet
Europe's first commercially successful steamship and the foundation of a Clydeside tradition.
Authors' Collection

boat... constructed to go by wind-power, and steam, for carrying passengers on the Clyde' it could be forgiven for not seeing in this event the dawning of the age of steam navigation and the rise of what would be for generations Glasgow and the Clyde's defining industry.

What the *Comet* brought in the first instance to the river traffic on the Clyde was, above all, a much-needed regularity and reliability. It had long been possible to travel, under sail, from the centre of the city to the towns down-river by what were referred to as 'fly-boats'. The disadvantage of these vessels was that faced with adverse winds (and the Clyde flows westward into the prevailing wind), it often took a great many hours to reach port. The alternative for travellers to the towns and ports of the lower Clyde was to take a stagecoach over rough and ill-maintained roads. The *Comet* for the first time offered a reliable and reasonably swift journey, reaching Greenock in four hours. In the early weeks of *Comet*'s operation the advertised service to Helensburgh was, however, completed by a passage on a sailing ship from Greenock.

Helensburgh was not chosen as the final destination by accident or caprice. Henry Bell had built and then ran the Baths Inn there and catered for the fashionable taste for therapeutic sea-bathing. But the success of his enterprise was handicapped by the difficulties his clients faced in reaching Helensburgh, some 25 miles by road, or perhaps as much as 12 hours by river, from Glasgow.

Bell's background was not as an hotelier but as a practical engineer. Born in 1767 to a family of mill-wrights and mill-owners in Torphichen, West Lothian, he was apprenticed to the family trade but left to gain wider experience in a shipyard at Bo'ness, then worked with an engineer in the Lanarkshire coalfields and finally went to London to work for the great Scottish engineer, John Rennie, later engaging in major contracts such as the steam-powered Albion Flour Mills. This wide experience was, arguably, just what Bell needed to see his plan for steam navigation through to success; despite the negativity – where steam at sea was concerned – of many contemporary engineers of vastly greater reputation, such as his fellow-countryman James Watt.

Bell came back to Scotland and set up in business on his own account as a wright in Gorbals around 1791, eventually joining the Incorporation of Wrights in Glasgow in 1797. Bell had a varied practice, designing at least one church, building a flour mill at Partick, and working on mills

FIG. 5.2
Henry Bell
The talented, if financially unstable, owner and designer of the *Comet*.
Authors' Collection

for the textile industry in the Vale of Leven. It is probable – but reliable documentation is scanty – that throughout these years an early interest in steam navigation developed, and there is an account of Bell and Robert Fulton paying a visit to the *Charlotte Dundas,* laid-up at Falkirk, around the year 1805.

In 1809 and 1810 Bell conducted scale-model experiments in which he satisfied himself that steam propulsion was possible; as he wrote himself: 'I succeeded so far in my views, that I was fully convinced a vessel of any size could be wrought by steam.' Part of Bell's real significance among the many experimenters with steam at sea was that he always had a far-ranging, indeed visionary, sense of what could be achieved and his ambitions for steamships went well beyond the idea of auxiliary propulsion or mere service on rivers and canals. Indeed, when the best and most informed opinion saw steamboats as confined to rivers, bays and canals, Bell was sending a lengthened *Comet* through some of the roughest waters around the coast on a pioneering service to Fort William, and making plans for a steamboat service to Stornoway in Lewis. As early as 1824 he was outlining plans for a steamboat service between Britain and India. Even his design of the *Comet,* with his inclusion of cabins with beds – hardly needed for a journey to Greenock – suggests that he saw much greater potential for the *Comet* than just a river ferry service.

Bell's new ship was faced with initial suspicion. In a letter of 1824 he says, in his characteristically idiosyncratic spelling:

> … but the pradiges [prejudice] was so grate against Steam Boat Navigation by the hue and cry of the fly boat pepul and coach contractors – that for the first six months very few wold venture their preshious lives in her – but in course of the winter sayson as she played all year she began to gain credit.[1]

A few years later a Glasgow writer, James Cleland, noted that before the coming of the steamships it was doubtful if more than 50 people a day travelled between Glasgow and Greenock, but now between 400 and 500 a day made the journey. Bell had launched not just a ship but a transport revolution. Soon travel for pleasure as well as for practical business reasons became a growth industry.

The *Comet* was soon joined by other steamships on the river and Bell

---

[1] National Library of Scotland Acc. 12402

was to complain that as soon as steamships were seen to be practical and profitable, larger concerns with more financial resources had come on the scene and invested in larger and more powerful ships. Soon the *Comet* was outclassed on the Clyde and as Bell wrote later, in the second year of her service (1813), he:

> ... made her a Jaunting Boat all over the coasts of England, Ireland and Scotland to show the Habitants the advantages and quality of steam boat Navigation to the other moad of sailing... I erected several other steamboats and opened up the most part of all the different stashions whair steam boats plays in Scotland and all this single handed.[2]

One of these jaunts was to Leith. Bell sailed the *Comet* through the Forth and Clyde Canal, had her taken into his old employer's shipyard, Shaw and Hart at Bo'ness, for a refit and then on to Leith. The enterprising Bell combined the passage from Bo'ness to Leith with a moneymaking opportunity by running the first ever steamboat excursion on the Forth between the two ports, for the single fare of seven shillings and sixpence. On 24 May 1813 the *Edinburgh Evening Courant* reported that:

> The *Comet* of Helensburgh, a vessel worked by steam, and the first of the kind ever seen in this quarter, is at present lying in Leith Harbour.[3]

Thereafter the *Comet* commenced a regular service between Grangemouth at the end of the Forth and Clyde Canal and Newhaven outside Edinburgh, a service designed to connect with the Canal Company's horse-towed canal passage boats from Glasgow. This, for a time, proved to be a popular and well-supported service, which was encouraged by the Canal Company as a valued adjunct to their services. However, within a few years Bell found that his Clyde experience was being replicated on the Forth and larger and better vessels were winning away his passengers.

In 1818 Bell began to think seriously about running services to the West Highlands of Scotland. However, as she was the *Comet* was not ideally suited to this route, so in 1819 he had her beached at Helensburgh, cut in two and lengthened from 42 feet to 73 feet 10 inches, and at this time she was possibly re-engined. The original three horsepower engine was certainly replaced but whether at this stage or earlier is now unclear. William Thomson, the resident engineer of the Crinan Canal, wrote:

---

[2] Ibid
[3] Glasgow *Mechanics Magazine* 5 February 1835

Mr Bell made his appearance with his *Comet* under the best repair she was capable of, and with such improvements as the engine and machinery would admit of, in August 1819.[4]

At 9am on Thursday 2 September 1819, *Comet* sailed from Glasgow to Fort William via Greenock, Gourock, Rothesay, Tarbert, Loch Gilp, Crinan, Easdale, Oban and Port Appin, commencing a weekly service to the West Highlands, which would be maintained in all but the worst months of winter, when the schedule would drop to a fortnightly one. Bell's finances were never of the soundest: he had indeed mortgaged the Baths Inn to finance his original steam experiments and the building of the *Comet,* and during 1819 and 1820 he sold off shares in the ship to a wide range of investors, including West Highland landowners such as Sir Ewen Cameron of Fassfern and Colonel McLean of Ardgour, as well as merchants in Fort William. Matters were put on a more formal basis and the loose co-partnership that now owned the *Comet* would be transformed into the 'Comet Steam Boat Company'. Bell himself would become superintendent of the company, which was due to be formed on 1 January 1821.

Throughout 1819 and 1820 *Comet* traded successfully and profitably for Bell and his investors – in a letter of December 1819 to a Highland landlord, Sir Hugh Innes of Lochalsh, Bell claimed that since putting the Comet into service to Fort William she had covered all her expenses and made a profit of 10 per cent on her valuation, which he puts at £1,800 at least.

However, Bell's luck was about to run out. *Comet* sailed on 4 December 1820 for Fort William on her fortnightly winter schedule – 41 passengers travelled north with her and she was due to return from Fort William on Monday 11 December. This round trip seems to have been plagued with incident – she struck a rock in Loch Linnhe and was beached to allow repairs to be made. The return journey was delayed and an overnight stop was made at Oban on 14 December – clearly the ship was in difficulties because the account book for the *Comet* shows payments to four men for pumping the vessel that night. On Friday 15 December she left Oban in bad weather, passed down the Firth of Lorne in a violent snowstorm, but when rounding Craignish Point to the *Dorus Mor* and the entrance to the Crinan Canal she ran on to rocks at Craignish. A contemporary newspaper report tells of her end:

---

[4]   Morris, Edward, *The Life of Henry Bell*, Blackie & Sons, Glasgow, 1844

the *Comet* steam-boat… while passing through Dorishmore, at the point of Craignish Rock, was struck with a strong gust of wind, which laid her on her beam ends; and in ten minutes, owing to the great current of tide and high seas and wind, was laid broadside on the rocks. Every exertion was made for the landing of passengers and men, which was safely accomplished. On Saturday morning she was a complete wreck…

The ship apparently split in two at the point where she had been lengthened the previous year. Some sources have suggested that Bell had economised by using unsuitable and unseasoned timber for this lengthening and the total loss of the *Comet* has been attributed to this cause. If, as seems likely, Bell only intended to operate the *Comet* for a short time on the West Highland route, and he was reported to be in Fort William discussing the financing of a new and larger ship in December 1820 and probably travelled south on the *Comet*'s last voyage, this may not have been as irresponsible a decision as it may at first appear.

So *Comet*'s short, if eventful, life ended a little over eight years after her first commercial journey, and by her end she had been seriously outclassed by many competitive steamers. Bell was never to win the financial success that his pioneering efforts deserved and might have been expected to attract. From 1812 to his death in 1830 he was faced with chronic financial problems, partly caused by his own poor money management. Why, then, does *Comet* figure in this list of great Scottish ships?

Although she may not have broken new ground – the basic problems had been solved by Miller and Symington, to say nothing of the American Robert Fulton – *Comet* set the pattern for future developments in steam at sea, and this primacy was acknowledged at the time as well as with the advantage of hindsight. One of the pieces of evidence for this is the decision of the company that owned the *Comet* to replace her with a new and larger vessel, ordered from Andrew Lang of Dumbarton, even before the December 1820 wreck. This new ship was also to be called *Comet* – clearly the commercial advantages of capitalising on the brand name was not lost on the owners, and the compliment to Bell, by this point no longer a shareholder and merely the marine superintendent of the company, was obvious.

Equally significant was a letter written in 1825 and signed by all the principal marine engineers on the Clyde:

We, the undersigned engineers in Glasgow, having been employed for some time past in making engines for steam-vessels in Glasgow, certify that the machinery and paddles used by Henry Bell, in his steam-boat, the *Comet,* in 1812, have undergone little or no alteration, notwithstanding several attempts of ingenious persons to improve them.

Signed

Hugh & Robert Baird

John Neilson

David Napier

Robert Napier

David McArthur

Claud Girdwood & Co,

Murdoch & Cross

William McAndrew

William Watson[5]

This statement of the essential similarity of machinery 13 years after the *Comet* first sailed is significant because it comes from technically knowledgeable men, including David Napier, whose generosity to Bell's reputation is perhaps the more remarkable because Bell still, in 1825, owed him money for the *Comet*'s boiler.

Lest it be thought that these engineers were motivated by local chauvinism in their plaudits for Bell, consider the evidence of perhaps an even more famous engineer – no less a figure than Isambard Kingdom Brunel, who recognised Henry Bell's claim to priority and recognition. Bell's friend and first biographer, Edward Morris, called on Brunel when raising funds for Bell's support. Brunel contributed generously to the subscription but expressed the view that the British government should have paid Bell £1,000 a year on the grounds that Bell had 'worked nobly for his country; he accomplished what others had failed in'. Brunel also expressed the same sentiment more pithily:

Bell did what we engineers all failed in – he gave us the sea steamer; his scheming was Britain's steaming.

So expert contemporaries realised and acknowledged Bell's contribution

---

[5] Morris, Edward, *The Life of Henry Bell*, Blackie & Sons, Glasgow, 1844

with the *Comet* to have been one of the greatest significance, and indeed the remarkable story of the Clyde's rise to dominance in the world of shipbuilding and marine engineering starts with that little wooden-hulled ship puffing its way from the Broomielaw to the Baths Inn.

One hundred years after that first voyage by 'the power of Wind, Air and Steam', Glasgow, the Clyde and Scotland marked the centenary with every form of celebration imaginable – a review of merchant shipping was held off Greenock, a squadron of the Home Fleet was in attendance, numerous magazine and newspaper features, lectures and exhibitions, fireworks and luncheons, public holidays and flag-flying all testified to the lasting impact that *Comet* had had on the world. When the dignitaries sailed down-river on MacBrayne's *Columba* they would pass, between the Broomielaw and Greenock, 29 shipyards with 175 vessels building or fitting-out in them. Ships of every size and type from Cunard's giant *Aquitania* building at John Brown's at Clydebank, the *Empress of Asia* and *Empress of Russia* for Canadian Pacific building at Fairfield, Govan, down to the humble dredgers at Lobnitz, Renfrew. As we approach the bicentenary the Clyde is no longer lined with shipyards and thronged with shipping, nor are Glasgow's streets lined with the head offices of shipping lines, so the influence and the impact of the *Comet* may be less obvious. But while the concept of 'Clyde-built' still has resonance, and while the emotional connection of Scotland to ships and the sea remains, the first commercial steamship in Europe and the foundation of a once great Scottish industry deserves to be remembered with pride.

CHAPTER 6

ps *Britannia* (1840–80)

IN 1838 THE paddle steamer *Sirius* made the first transatlantic voyage under continuous steam power – earlier steamers had only used their engines for part of the journey. However, the *Sirius* did not signal the start of a regular steam service and most traffic across the Atlantic continued to be operated by sailing ships. An important part of this traffic was the Royal Mail service between Britain, Canada and the United States – this was in the hands of fast packet ships operating out of Falmouth under an Admiralty contract.

The idea of a regular scheduled steam service across the Atlantic had been raised on a number of occasions and in 1833 the Glasgow marine engineer Robert Napier (1791–1876) had produced highly detailed plans for a London businessman, Patrick Wallace, who was investigating the possibility of starting just such a steamer service between Liverpool and North America. Nothing came of Wallace's idea, although Napier's work was put to good effect when he supplied the engines for the Thames-built *British Queen* in 1839 – this ship proved successful on the Atlantic route but for other reasons the owners withdrew from the service.

In 1838 the Admiralty expressed willingness to offer a contract for an Atlantic mail service by steamer and Samuel Cunard (1787–1865), a businessman from Halifax, Nova Scotia, obtained a provisional contract and came to Britain to find the means of fulfilling the terms of the contract. The mail contract was potentially lucrative and would subsidise the operation of a fleet of steamers, which could also carry passengers and light cargoes; however, the penalty clauses for lateness or failure to meet departure dates were high and the ships built for the service would require to be fast, rugged and reliable.

Amongst Cunard's business interests was the representation of the Honourable East India Company in Halifax and one of his early calls in London was on James C. Melvill, the Secretary of the East India Company. Melvill knew Robert Napier's work well – Napier had supplied the Company with an excellent steamer for the Indian mail service, the

Berenice, and Melvill recommended that Cunard's best plan was to put his requirements before Napier and take his advice.

On 25 February 1839 Cunard wrote to his Glasgow agents asking that they should approach Napier and the shipbuilder John Wood for an estimate for the building of one or two 300 horse power, 800 ton wooden-hulled ships. At this stage in Napier's career he was principally a marine engineer but he also acted as contract manager, designing ships and placing building orders with yards around the Clyde, chiefly the Port Glasgow yard of John Wood, builder of Henry Bell's *Comet* and reputed to be the finest builder on the river. Cunard travelled north and met with Napier at his Glasgow home, Lancefield House, in March 1839. A swift arrangement was made to build three ships of the desired size at a cost of £30,000 each, and Cunard left for London. By the time of his next trip north in mid-March, he was faced with a problem. Napier had concluded that larger and more powerful steamers would be needed to ensure the success of the project and proposed 960 ton, 375 horsepower ships, at a cost of £32,000. The new contract was less beneficial to Napier but

FIG. 6.1
Britannia in ice at Boston
The first Cunarder being cut free from an iced-up Boston Harbour.
Authors' Collection

his reputation was at stake and he felt that he would be blamed for any shortcomings in the ships he would deliver. Samuel Cunard, although concerned at the rising costs, was shrewd enough to know that he was getting a good deal and signed a contract with Napier for the three uprated ships on 18 March 1839.

Cunard wrote to Napier from London on 21 March to say that the Admiralty and the Treasury were delighted with the revised specification, and also mentioned that he had encountered considerable prejudice against Scottish shipbuilders – he had been told that: 'You will neither have substantial work nor completed on time.'[1] Napier wrote to assure him that 'I cannot and will not admit of anything being done or introduced into these engines but what I am satisfied with is sound and good.'[2]

The relationship between Napier and Cunard was soon on a warm and friendly basis. By April 1839 Cunard was closing his business letters to Glasgow with good wishes to Napier's wife and family.

Cunard shared with Napier his calculations on the costs and potential profits of the project. Writing from London on 11 April 1839, he laid out the likely costs:

Coal at 1.25 tons per hour	£17,640
Wages and provisions for crew	£10,500
Wear and tear	£10,000
Interest and Insurance	£10,000
Sundries to cover port charges and agency	£10,860
Allowance for branch boats in Canada	£10,000
Total	**£69,000**

The Income was estimated as:

38 1st class passengers each way at £25 net profit	£36,000
15 2nd class passengers each way	£10,800
Troops	£2,000
Fine goods 50 tons each outward	
Passage at £5 per tonne	£6,000
Allowance from Government	£55,000
Total	**£109,800**
Surplus	£40,800[3]

---

[1] Napier/Cunard Correspondence, Glasgow Museum of Transport
[2] Ibid
[3] Ibid

These calculations were based on three ships of 960 tons each, but Robert Napier was not finished yet – at this time he was completing the engines for the *British Queen*, which was bigger and more powerful than the Cunard ships – and he advised Cunard to again increase the size and power. Not unnaturally Cunard was reluctant, as he was finding great difficulty in obtaining financial backing for the existing scheme, much less a more expensive scheme. The British base for the service would be Liverpool, geographically well suited to a service to Canada and the United States; however, the mercantile community of Liverpool was slow to invest in Cunard's scheme, in part at least because of prejudice against Scottish builders. Cunard was supported in his view of the adequacy of the revised specification by the Admiralty but on consulting Melvill of the East India Company he was advised that Napier knew much more about long-distance steam navigation than did the Admiralty and that he should go to Glasgow and put all the financial and technical issues before Napier and see what Napier could do to assist him. Cunard took this advice and came north to Glasgow for a critical meeting.

In addition to his other interests, Napier was a shareholder in the City of Glasgow Steam Packet Company – a line trading between the Clyde and the Mersey. Napier put together a group of friends and business associates connected to the City of Glasgow Company, and other merchants and shipping agents, and swiftly managed to raise £270,000 capital to float the rather lengthily titled British and North American Royal Mail Steam Packet Company – fortunately usually known as the Cunard Line.

Cunard himself was the largest shareholder, subscribing £55,000. Robert Napier invested £6,000. Management would be in the hands of Napier's friends, the McIver brothers, ship managers based in Liverpool. Napier's influence was strongly marked, the Cunard livery of red funnels was based on the colour scheme Napier had adopted for his own Scottish steamers; more significantly the final contract was again altered to meet Napier's views about the requirements for a reliable and profitable Atlantic service. The three ships mentioned in the 18 March contract became four ships, their size increased from 960 tons to 1,150 tons, their engine power from 375 horsepower to 440 horsepower.

Cunard had not only to concern himself with the procurement of ships and raising capital, he had also to keep his Admiralty funders happy. In April 1839 he wrote to Napier asking for plans of the new ships to show to Sir Edward Parry, Controller of the Steam Department, and to Mr Wood (presumably Charles Wood, 1st Secretary to the Admiralty): 'I want to make the boats look as large as possible, you may also add the extreme length overall.'[4]

The Admiralty and the Treasury eventually accepted the advantages of a four-ship fleet and Cunard's annual subsidy was raised to £60,000. However, the terms were strict – if a ship was late leaving harbour or delayed or diverted on passage for a reason deemed unacceptable by the naval officer on board in charge of the mails, then a penalty of £100 per incident was payable. If a scheduled service left more than 12 hours late, a penalty of £500 was payable, with a further £500 for every further period of 12 hours. In the state of marine engineering in 1839 this put a very high premium on Napier's engineering abilities.

A contract of this size was more than John Wood's yard could handle in the time allowed and three ships went to other yards around the Clyde.

SHIP	YARD	LOCATION
Acadia	John Wood	Port Glasgow
Britannia	Robert Duncan	Greenock
Caledonia	Charles Wood	Dumbarton
Columbia	Robert Steele	Greenock

Other yards might be used, but Cunard placed his confidence in John Wood and Napier;

> let who will build the vessels Mr Wood and you must look to their being well done, I rest my faith in you two and know that I shall not be disappointed.[5]

On 8 February a local correspondent of *The Times* reported the launch of the *Britannia* by Miss Isabella Napier, Robert's daughter:

> Her length from taffrail to figure-head is 230 feet, the breadth of her beam is 34½ feet, and the depth of her hold 22 feet 6 inches. She is to be propelled by two engines, each 220-horse power, and when put

---

[4] Ibid

[5] Ibid

to sea will be succeeded by three other ships of the same dimension and similar constructions, all intended, as we have said, to carry the mails, passengers, etc., between Liverpool and North America, a scheme, it will be remembered which was originated by the Hon. S. Cunard, of Halifax, Nova Scotia, who with a small party of influential gentlemen in Glasgow, is associated in this great undertaking. The vessel's hull and machinery are constructed under the direction and superintendence of Mr Robert Napier, of the Vulcan Foundry, Glasgow; and when we mention this gentleman's name as connected with such a work we give a sufficient guarantee that, when completed, nothing better will be found in the kingdom. The accommodation of the vessel is provided on an improved and magnificent scale, the cabin below deck being fitted up with spacious and well-ventilated state-rooms.

Even at this early stage in the career of the man who became known as the 'Father of Clyde Shipbuilding' Napier was renowned for his workmanship. As an engine builder and contract manager he had successfully broken into the closed circle of London contractors to the Admiralty and the East India Company and had provided a much-admired trio of ships for the Dundee, Perth and London Shipping Company's service between the Tay and the Thames. As ships increased in size and engines in power and weight, the practical limits of the wooden shipbuilding, so expertly carried out by John Wood, Charles Wood, Robert Duncan and their contemporaries on the Clyde, were being reached and Napier, seeing where progress was leading, acquired land at Govan and laid out his own shipyard to handle the new technology. The first ship to come from his yard was launched in 1843. It was not simply Napier's prescient adoption of iron construction that won him his prestigious title, but the large number of prominent shipbuilders and engineers who trained under him or who worked for him – men like James Thomson, later to found his own firm, later known as John Brown & Co.; William Denny of Denny Bros of Dumbarton fame; and John Elder, who later founded the marine engineering firm of Randolph, Elder and the shipyard of John Elder and Co., later to be better known as the Fairfield Shipbuilding and Engineering Co.

By 12 June the *Glasgow Herald* could report that three Cunarders were lying at Broomielaw Quay in the centre of the city; *Britannia* readying for her trial trip, *Acadia* and *Caledonia* getting their engines put on board, and *Columbia* was reported to be due to launch in a few days. *Britannia*'s trial trip was successful and she sailed to Liverpool from Greenock on 25 June, completing the passage in less than 17 hours.

The London *Times* on 22 June 1840 advertised, under the heading 'Steam from Liverpool to Boston', the first scheduled sailing of *Britannia* at noon on 4 July – a date probably determined as much by the Post Office's schedule rather than any desire to pay a compliment to the Independence Day of the United States. It was also, coincidentally, Samuel Cunard's 53rd birthday. The four ships were listed in the advertisement with their respective captains:

Britannia	Captain Robert Ewing
Acadia	Captain Robert Miller
Caledonia	Captain Richard Cleland
Columbia	Captain Henry Woodruff

Miller and Cleland would be with Cunard for some time, the others only seem to have completed a round trip each. It seems probable that Ewing and Woodruff were temporary appointments, experienced steamer masters put in place while permanent appointments were being made. Henry Woodruff was Captain of the Antwerp steamer *Princess Victoria*, and Captain Ewing was master of one of the Dundee, Perth & London Company's steamers. As Napier had been closely concerned with that company's move into steam it is probable that Ewing was borrowed for the *Britannia*'s first voyage through the agency of Napier.

Napier had offered to recommend suitable captains but Cunard noted that the Admiralty might want to nominate masters. In the event, two of the four named above, Miller and Woodruff, were lieutenants in the Royal Navy. The peacetime navy had far more officers than it could use and there was nothing unusual in a half-pay officer without a post finding employment in the Merchant Service. Ewing and Cleland do not appear in the navy list. Cleland seems to have been employed by Napier before *Caledonia* was ready. In January 1840 Napier sent him to London on what seems to have been a piece of industrial espionage, to check up on potential competitors. Cunard, writing to Napier on 30 January, acknowledged receipt of a letter delivered by Captain Cleland and noted:

I think you have acted very prudently in sending him on the mission and I have no doubt but the information he has collected will be very useful. He appears to have taken much pains in collecting the information.[6]

The fares for the passage were advertised – to Halifax 34 guineas (£35.70), and to Boston 38 guineas (£39.90). These prices included provisions and wine, although an additional guinea (£1.05) was payable to the steward. It is always hard to give an accurate idea of current and historic costs – one calculation using the retail price index suggests that the 38 guineas for a crossing to Boston equate to just over £2,500 at current prices. The Cunard crossing to Boston was more expensive than the sailing packets between London and New York, which advertised cabin passage at 25 guineas 'without wines, spirits etc.' – but presumably the reliability of the steamer service compensated for the extra cost.

Britannia was not a particularly fast ship, with an operational speed of 9 knots, but her great plus point was reliability and the end of dependence on winds. Britannia and her sister ships, like all ocean-going steamships then and for many years after, were fully rigged as sailing ships and used sail, whenever the wind served, as auxiliary power. The steam engines of the period were quite inefficient, at least as compared to later compound marine steam engines – the double, triple and quadruple expansion engines that re-used steam at successively lower pressures, allowing greater power and fuel economy.

Britannia sailed for Halifax and Boston on Saturday 4 July and completed the journey to Boston in 14¼ days, including a stopover for discharge of mails at Halifax. The Novascotian newspaper in Halifax observed: 'She is a noble-looking ship, fitted up, we understand, in a comfortable, efficient but plain style' and commenting on her 12½ day crossing to Halifax, observed that:

> Twelve days may well be considered as a minimum, which is scarcely susceptible of diminution, and of which diminution should scarcely be wished. He who is not satisfied with travelling, steadily, 250 miles in a natural day, scarcely deserves satisfaction.

Among the passengers on the first crossing was Samuel Cunard himself,

---

[6] Napier/Cunard Correspondence, Glasgow Museum of Transport

who received a warm welcome at Boston by the people of Massachusetts, who presented him with a silver cup to mark the start of a regular service between their city and the United Kingdom. The Boston Cup has since that time always been carried on the flagship of the Cunard fleet and today is proudly displayed onboard *Queen Mary 2*.

Boston saw the arrival of *Britannia* as more than just an interesting incident in transport history – it was recognised as a major development in the city's economy and its rise to commercial prominence. The Rev. Ezra S. Gannett, a Boston Unitarian minister, preaching on 19 July in the Federal Street Meeting House, reflected on the consequences that greater contact with Europe would bring, on the way that steam commerce would bind Britain and the USA together and reduce the risk of war and rivalry. He observed:

> I confess that no event which has occurred since the commencement of the present century seems to me to have involved more important consequences to this city, than are likely to flow from the establishment of regular and efficient steam communication between the capital of New England and the great commercial island – the maritime threshold, if I may so style it, of the Old World.[1]

The connection between the city of Boston and the Cunard Line would be a close one – in 1844 *Britannia* was due to sail for Liverpool on 1 February but found herself ice-bound by unusually severe weather – her departure was delayed until 2 February and her passage out of the harbour required a passageway of some seven or eight miles to be cut through the ice (see illustration 6.1). This work was undertaken at the expense of the citizens of Boston, who valued their regular Cunard steamer connection. However, the propensity of Boston harbour to freeze over was perhaps one reason why Cunard, by 1847, had switched part of their services to New York, although Boston continued to be a Cunard port into the 20th century.

As Cunard's other ships became available, a regular fortnightly service became possible. In the four winter months – November to February – only one crossing each direction per month was thought necessary. The last

---

[1] Gannett, Ezra S, *A Sermon delivered in the Federal Street Meeting-House in Boston, July 19 1840*, Joseph Dowe, Boston, Mass., 1840

of the four ships, *Columbia*, came into service with a sailing from Liverpool on 5 January 1841. The press carried regular reports of the speed and reliability of *Britannia* and the other Cunard liners – generally the route from Liverpool to Boston, even with the few hours spent discharging mails and passengers at Halifax, Nova Scotia, was operated in less time than the *British Queen* between Portsmouth and New York, or the *Great Western* between Bristol and New York. The newspapers were, of course, intensely interested in the speed of crossing because in those years before Atlantic telegraph cables they were dependent on these ships for the latest newspapers and intelligence from the United States and Canada.

Britannia may have been a well-built and reliable ship but her most famous passenger, Charles Dickens, who, with his wife, took passage in her to America on Tuesday 4 January 1842, was distinctly unimpressed. Dickens was already internationally famous as the author of *Oliver Twist, Nicholas Nickleby* and *The Pickwick Papers*. In a letter to his brother, Frederick, written from Liverpool after a preliminary inspection of the accommodation, he complained:

> Our cabin is something immensely smaller than you can possibly picture to yourself. Neither of the portmanteaus could by any mechanical contrivance be got into it. When the door is open you can't turn round. When it's shut you can't put on a clean shirt, or take off a dirty one. When it's day, it's dark. When it's night it's cold.[2]

Dickens vividly described the rigours of his passage to Boston in the opening chapters of his *American Notes*. He perhaps had become reconciled to the limited accommodation in his state-room, in part because of the adjacent 'ladies' cabin', which, with only a few female passengers on board, Dickens and his wife would be able to use – and which he described as 'a really comfortable room… well-lighted, sofa'd, mirrored, and so forth.' He describes with a genuinely Dickensian relish the preparations for departure, and it is fascinating to catch a glimpse of the routine of an 1842 Cunarder:

> … one party of men were 'taking in the milk', or, in other words, getting the cow on board; and another were filling the icehouses to the

---

[2] Dickens, Charles, *Letters of Charles Dickens,* Clarendon Press, Oxford, 1966–2002

very throat with fresh provisions; with butcher's-meat and garden-stuff, pale sucking-pigs, calves' heads in scores, beef, veal and pork, and poultry out of all proportion; and others were busy coiling ropes and busy with oakum yarns; and others were lowering heavy packages into the hold; and the purser's head was barely visible as it loomed in a state of exquisite perplexity from the midst of a vast pile of passengers' luggage; and there seemed to be nothing going on anywhere, or uppermost in the mind of anybody, but preparations for this mighty voyage.

At last everything is on board and on Tuesday 4 January *Britannia* leaves Liverpool. At first the weather is calm, but...

It is the third morning. I am awakened out of my sleep by a dismal shriek from my wife, who demands to know whether there is any danger. I rouse myself and look out of bed. The water-jug is plunging and leaping like a lively dolphin; all the smaller items are afloat, except my shoes, which are stranded on a carpet-bag, high and dry, like a couple of coal-barges. Suddenly I see them spring into the air, and behold the looking-glass, which is nailed to the wall, sticking fast upon the ceiling. At the same time the door entirely disappears, and a new one is opened in the floor. Then I begin to comprehend that the state-room is standing on its head.

Before it is possible to make any arrangement at all compatible with this novel state of things, the ship rights. Before one can say 'Thank Heaven!' she wrongs again.[3]

Dickens asks a passing steward what was wrong and is told merely that there is 'rather a heavy sea on, Sir, and a head-wind'. In fact, as the chief engineer later admits, the weather was particularly rough and even crew members had succumbed to seasickness, the paddle boxes were torn off and lifeboats smashed. Some idea of the conditions is suggested by the fact that passage took 18 days from Liverpool to Boston, significantly longer than the 14½ days of the maiden voyage back in 1840 – but it was January, in the North Atlantic.

To add to what had been a trying voyage *Britannia* was briefly, due to

---

[3] Dickens, Charles, *American Notes,* Oxford University Press, London, 1957

FIG. 6.2
Charles Dickens
Portrayed at around the age of his January crossing to America in *Britannia*.
Authors' Collection

the pilot's error, stranded on a mud bank at the approach to Halifax harbour, but Halifax and Boston were both reached without loss of life and Mr Dickens could set off on his triumphant tour of North America. However, on the last day of the journey the *Britannia*'s passengers formed a committee (Chairman the Earl of Mulgrave, Secretary and Treasurer Charles Dickens Esq.) to raise a subscription to buy a silver plate for Captain John Hewitt in appreciation of his 'great ability and skill under circumstances of much difficulty and danger; and as a feeble token of their lasting gratitude'. Fifty pounds was raised and a silver pitcher, salver and goblets were presented to the captain at a meeting in the Tremont Theatre, Boston. Despite his appreciation of the captain's skill, Dickens decided to make the return voyage from America in a sailing ship – apparently more on the grounds of comfort than on concerns of safety.

It is hard not to feel that Dickens somewhat exaggerated the hardships and dangers of the passage – he had, of course, no previous experience of an Atlantic voyage and had hardly chosen the best time of year for his first crossing. He was also anxious, as are all authors, to sell his book and a highly coloured account of the perils of the sea was not unhelpful to that end. Early steamship crossings of the Atlantic were, admittedly, dangerous and several of Cunard's later rivals had ships sink with all hands, disappear or hit icebergs – Cunard, however, had an excellent safety record and although ships had accidents – the *Britannia* would run aground again off Newfoundland in September 1847 – there were no passengers lost. Excellence of design, conservatism in operation, and insistence on rigorous quality standards were features on which Cunard and Napier were at one and were largely responsible for this record.

The North Atlantic service was fiercely competitive and hardly had Samuel Cunard got his four steamers running than he was back to Napier to order new ships. During the next decade Napier and the shipyards of the Clyde would produce another eight ships for Cunard – each a little larger and more powerful than the previous batch – Napier's views on size, power and quality continued to be influential.

YEAR	SHIP	YARD	TONNAGE	HORSEPOWER
1842	*Hibernia*	Robert Steele	1,353	473
1844	*Cambria*	Robert Steele	1,353	473
1847	*America*	Robert Steele	1,756	630
1847	*Europa*	John Wood	1,764	648
1848	*Canada*	Robert Steele	1,756	648
1848	*Niagara*	Robert Steele	1,756	630
1850	*Africa*	Robert Steele	2,128	768
1850	*Asia*	Robert Steele	2,128	768

The Cunard Company continued to be conservative in demanding wooden ships, despite Napier having opened an iron shipbuilding yard at Govan. Not until the beautiful *Persia* of 1855 did Cunard order an iron ship from Napier and the Company maintained its preference for paddle wheels over screw propulsion up to the *Scotia* of 1861.

Soon the first generation of Cunarders became outclassed and surplus to requirements. *Britannia* arrived in Liverpool from her last Atlantic crossing on 28 December 1848. In February 1849 *Britannia* and *Acadia* were in the Coburg Docks, Liverpool, being converted into warships following their sale to the German Federation. *Britannia* was equipped with nine guns manufactured at the Woolwich Arsenal and renamed *Barbarossa*. She saw action in June 1849 in the North Sea in the war with Denmark over Schleswig-Holstein. In April 1852, following the break-up of the German Federation Navy, she was transferred to the navy of the Kingdom of Prussia. She served in that navy until 1880, when she was sunk as a target for torpedo experiments.

Small, slow, and if Dickens is to be believed, uncomfortable, *Britannia* may not have borne much comparison with later and more luxurious Cunarders like the *Queen Mary* or the *Queen Elizabeth II* (see Chapter 14), but her place in maritime history is secure and her sturdy frame and mechanical reliability is a lasting credit to the skills of the Clyde that gave her birth, and to the pioneering vision of Samuel Cunard and Robert Napier.

CHAPTER 7

The Puffer (1856–)

She wass chust sublime. A gold bead oot of my own pocket, four
men and a derrick, a water-butt and a pan-loaf in the fo'c'sle. My
bonny wee *Vital Spark*.[1]

SO NEIL MUNRO'S Para Handy described his beloved command, the
puffer, *Vital Spark*, in the first of the series of short stories that made this
humdrum workhorse of the Clyde and West Highlands, 'aal hold, with the
boiler behind', into a Scottish, and international, icon. The skipper went on
to exclaim with pardonable, if excessive, enthusiasm:

Oh, man she wass the beauty! She wass chust sublime! She should
be carryin' nothing but gentry for passengers, or nice genteel luggage
for the shooting lodges, but there they would be spoilin' her and
rubbin' all the pent off her with their coals, and sand, and whunstone,
and oak bark, and timber, and trash like that.[2]

It was precisely to carry coals and sand and timber 'and trash like that'
that the puffer or steam lighter was developed to replace the sailing smacks
and gabbarts that had previously sustained the freight trade of the West
Highlands. They carried, in addition to Para Handy's catalogue of unde-
sirable cargoes, products such as grain to the island distilleries and whisky
back to the Lowlands. The sailing smacks and the puffers both reflected the
traditional Celtic view of the sea as a link, not a barrier. As we have seen
in Chapter 2, the early ships of the West coast, the curragh and the birlinn,
linked together isolated communities that were hard to reach by land, so,
into the second half of the 20th century, it was ships, not road vehicles
that carried bulk cargoes and household necessities into and out of the
West Highlands. Even in the years of decline of the puffer trade a major
source of work for these ships was in servicing 'coal clubs' – cooperatives
formed by Highland and Island communities to buy their winter's fuel
in bulk, in a puffer-load, have it delivered to a harbour or beach, unload
it as a community task and carry it back to their individual homes.

[1] Munro, Neil, *Complete Para Handy*, Birlinn, Edinburgh, 1992
[2] Ibid

The origins of the puffer can be traced back to 1856 when the Forth and Clyde Canal iron lighter *Thomas*, originally designed to be towed by horses, was fitted with an engine driving a screw propeller. This experiment was successful and in 1857 the first purpose-built steam lighter *Glasgow*, the first in the long puffer line, was launched at Kelvin Dock on the Canal from Swan's yard. The popular nickname came from the sound of the exhaust of the simple, non-condensing engines of the early models venting up the funnel.

Three broad categories of puffer developed in the following years – the simplest were designed for use on the canal itself and as such did not require crew accommodation or cargo handling gear. These 'inside' boats carried cargoes such as pig iron from Grangemouth to the foundries and ironworks in Falkirk, Kirkintilloch, Glasgow and other locations along the Canal. Timber, imported through Grangemouth, also formed a staple of the canal puffer's trade. A somewhat more seaworthy type, the 'shorehead boat', was developed for use on the Clyde estuary and the most advanced type, the 'outside boat', was designed to be able to trade out to the Hebrides. Para Handy's *Vital Spark* was of this latter type and indeed the skipper boasts that he was: 'not wan of your dry land sailors. I wass wance at Londonderry with her'.

The requirements for the 'outside' puffer were that it should be not much more than 66 feet in length and so able to pass through the locks of the Forth and Clyde Canal and should be able to beach safely at communities where there was no pier or dock, and there self-discharge her cargo (hence the derrick of Para Handy's description).

Of some 400 puffers built the majority came from yards on the Forth and Clyde Canal, such as Swan's at Kelvin Dock or the two shipbuilding yards in Kirkintilloch, J. & J. Hay's and P. MacGregor's. The inland burgh of Kirkintilloch, 15 miles up the canal from the sea-lock at Bowling, may be thought an unlikely centre of shipbuilding, but as the hub of the canal and an early interchange point for railway and canal traffic, it was from the 1870s until 1945 a significant centre of shipbuilding. Not only puffers but tugs, fishing boats and other craft were built at the two yards. MacGregor's yard closed in 1921, and although J. & J. Hay built their last puffer in 1945 – the *Chindit* for the associated puffer operator J. Hay & Sons Ltd. – they continued to overhaul and repair puffers in the middle of Kirkintilloch until 1961. The narrowness of the canal meant that Hay launched their puffers sideways into the canal, rather than by the more conventional stern first method.

The sea-going puffer, which became the typical model, evolved in the 1870s and by the end of the 19th century had taken on the form it was to retain until the end of the commercial puffer era. Typically around 66 feet long, it could carry around 100 tons of cargo and with her crew of four could deliver her cargo anywhere from the Clyde to Lewis, or across to Northern Ireland. The puffer also was not unknown on the east coast of Scotland and England.

As the years went on the puffer developed, wheelhouses appeared to give some shelter to the crew, and with the introduction of condensing engines, they ceased to puff, but the name stuck. Even when, in the years before the First World War, a fleet of coasters powered by internal combustion engines was ordered by a Glasgow company, the puffer hull shape was still used for most of these vessels and they were conventionally referred to as puffers. Six of these puffer-type motor vessels were ordered from the Kirkintilloch yard of Peter MacGregor & Sons.

Between the two world wars some larger puffers were built that exceeded the lock size of the Forth and Clyde Canal but which still fitted the 85 feet gauge of the Crinan Canal.

During the First World War requisitioned puffers had been found ideally suited to act as tenders to warships at Scapa Flow and other naval bases around Scotland. The puffer had often been used on the Clyde as a tender for large liners anchored at the Tail of the Bank, carrying coal out to refuel ships or to discharge their cargo and luggage; their use as naval auxiliaries was simply a development of this role.

So effective was the puffer in this naval role that, in the Second World War, the Admiralty ordered a fleet of puffer-type vessels – the victualling inshore craft, or VICs. Two of these were built at that traditional centre of puffer building, Hay's yard at Kirkintilloch, but most were built on the east coast of England. VICs served in all theatres of operations, being carried to overseas bases to serve in the traditional role of store carrier.

After the Second World War the decline of the puffer accelerated. Coal was rising in price and labour and other costs were escalating. Steam puffers were converted to diesel firing and gradually the fleets were reduced in size, although coasting vessels on the puffer lines continued to be built and operated.

The last substantial operator of puffers was the Glenlight Shipping Company, created in 1968 to operate the fleets of Hay-Hamilton, Ross & Marshall, and Irvine Shipping and Trading. However, one of the staple cargoes of the puffer trade – the supply of materials to the Islay distilleries – was soon to be lost to the new, and government-subsidised, roll-on roll-off car ferries, which operated between West Loch Tarbert and Islay. By the mid 1990s Glenlight had found it impossible to continue trading.

The *Eilean Eisdeal*, a 1941 vintage VIC built at Hull as VIC72, continued to operate for the Easdale Shipping Company and was the last puffer in general trade.

A few puffers are still to be found – *Spartan*, built in 1942 at Hay's yard in Kirkintilloch as VIC18, and after the war sold back to Hay's and traded for them until 1980 – is preserved at the Scottish Maritime Museum in Irvine. *Spartan* was converted to diesel engines in 1961 but a coal-fired puffer, VIC32, still survives. She operated holiday cruises out of Crinan until 2003 but a boiler failure took her out of commission. She has undergone restoration and resumed holiday sailing in the summer of 2007. VIC32 is now owned by the Puffer Preservation Trust and her future seems secure. The *Eilean Eisdeal* is now based at Inveraray, where it forms part of a group of attractions at the Maritime Museum and has been officially renamed *Vital Spark*.

The puffer's special place in the imagination and affections of many who never saw a cargo of coal unloaded on Tiree, or any of the many other cargoes that these little ships transported between the Clyde and hundred of west coast communities, is largely due to those two words 'Vital Spark'.

When the novelist Neil Munro created Para Handy, his puffer *Vital Spark* and the crew in January 1905, he could have had no idea that his creation would still be a potent element in Scottish culture and imagination 100 years later. The Para Handy stories were created for that most transient of media, a daily newspaper. Munro, by profession a journalist, had given up his staff post on the *Glasgow Evening News* to concentrate on his serious literary fiction. However, he continued to write two weekly columns for the paper. In one of these, 'The Looker-On', on 16 January 1905, a 'short, thick-set man with a red beard' and his soon-to-be-famous *Vital Spark*, 'the smartest boat in the tred' were introduced to a West of Scotland audience. The next year a collection of the stories was published in book form and for over 100 years the stories have never been out of print and continue to sell around 2,000 copies a year. In all, Munro wrote 100 stories about Para Handy, all of which are now collected in a complete and annotated edition.

So influential has been the impact of Para Handy and the *Vital Spark* that it seems impossible for any journalist to discuss shipping on the West Coast without making some reference to them. This must be partly due to the influence of the three television adaptations of the stories, starring Duncan Macrae (1959), Roddy McMillan (1965) and Gregor Fisher (1994) as the skipper; partly also to the 1954 film *The Maggie,* made by Alexander Mackendrick, which, though admitting no formal debt to Munro's creation, was surely influenced by it. Underlying the influence of all these adaptations, though, must remain the enduring charm and humour of the stories themselves.

The reality of the life of puffer crews was that it was a hard, dirty and at times dangerous job, but in Munro's tales these features are not emphasised and the prevailing impression is of freedom from routine, outside constraints and the humdrum workaday world, especially when the *Vital Spark* escapes into the idyllic world of Loch Fyne.

FIG. 7.1
The puffer *Saxon* at Millport 1965.
East Dunbartonshire Libraries

CHAPTER 8

HMS *Black Prince* (1861–1923)

WE ARE ACCUSTOMED to thinking of the River Clyde as the birthplace of so many of the Royal Navy's great ships of the late 19th and 20th centuries. Indeed, it almost seems as if there is a natural and inevitable connection between the river and the Navy – names like *Hood* and *Vanguard*, *Repulse* and *Renown* resound through naval history – and the Clyde, of course, produced vast quantities of naval ships of all types, from battleships down through aircraft carriers, cruisers, destroyers and submarines to tugs and dredgers. However, this connection is really only a product of the age of steam and iron.

Traditionally, the Royal Navy, in the age of wood and sail, had had its ships built and repaired in one of the Royal Naval Dockyards – Chatham, Portsmouth, Devonport or Pembroke; although some use was made of commercial builders, especially in times of emergency. These Royal dockyards were among the largest industrial complexes of their time and operated well enough in the sailing ship era. However, when steam propulsion came into the equation the dockyards did not initially have the expertise needed to fabricate engines and so, although wooden hulls continued to be built in the dockyards, the engines had to be manufactured at commercial marine engineering establishments.

These engineers tended to be based on the Thames and it proved to be a difficult job for engine builders outside London to break into this Admiralty market. This was partly due to London prejudice against 'country builders' and partly due to the very practical reason that a hull built in Chatham on the Thames or Portsmouth on the Solent was much more easily taken to Poplar or Limehouse than to the Clyde or the Tyne. It was also admittedly more convenient for the Admiralty to supervise work on the Thames than it was to supervise work at the other end of the country.

One Scottish engineer who struggled hard to win a share of Admiralty contracts was Robert Napier. In 1839 he won the contract to supply engines for *Vesuvius* and *Stromboli*, two wooden paddle sloops built at

Sheerness and Portsmouth respectively, and in 1844, having established his own iron shipbuilding yard at Govan, he won an Admiralty contract for three small iron gunboats – *Bloodhound*, *Jackal* and *Lizard*. These were the first iron warships for the Royal Navy – however, early iron construction was quickly shown to be unsuitable for fighting ships. Cast iron might have high tensile strength but was very brittle and when hit by a solid cannonball or an explosive shell it fractured badly and produced large quantities of lethal metal shards. A shell-damaged iron ship was also considerably more difficult to repair at sea than a wooden ship. An iron screw frigate, HMS *Simoom*, which Napier engined in 1849, was swiftly relegated to service as a troop ship because of this problem.

Through the period of the Crimean War (1853–6) Napier turned out iron ships and provided engines for wooden ones to meet the urgent demands of the Royal Navy in that war.

The Crimean War had seen a temporary Franco-British alliance but peace saw a reawakening of the traditional rivalry between Britain and France, and the presence of Napoleon III on the French throne awoke British suspicions of French imperial aggrandisement. The launch of the French ironclad *La Gloire* in 1859 was taken as a distinct threat to the comfortable British naval supremacy that had lasted since Trafalgar in 1805. *La Gloire* was seen as a huge leap forward, which rendered existing capital ships obsolete, in much the same way that Admiral Fisher's creation, in 1906, of the new all-big gun battleship HMS *Dreadnought* made existing battle fleets of limited value.

Press comment in 1859 speculated on the possibility of a French invasion. An elaborate and expensive series of fortifications were put in hand to protect key south coast naval installations such as Chatham, Portsmouth, Dover and Portland from the perceived French threat. To match the power of the new French battleship the Admiralty ordered two giant ships of 9,000 ton displacement *Warrior* and *Black Prince* – vastly larger than the three-decked steam- and sail-powered ships of the line that were still being built and which still resembled, apart from the addition of funnels, the *Victory* and other line of battle ships of the Trafalgar era. Quite how great a leap forward *Warrior* and *Black Prince* represented is indicated by the fact that they were 120 feet longer overall than the largest three-decker ship of the line.

This adherence to the 'wooden walls' was not entirely a matter of

Admiralty conservatism. A nation and a fleet, which had won supremacy in the age of sail and wood, would not lightly adopt a new technology which would render the old technology obsolescent. In the mid 19th century steam power alone could not yet propel a warship across the oceans of the world and had to be viewed as an auxiliary means of propulsion. The engines of the time were still inefficient and ships could not carry sufficient coal for long passages under power – *Black Prince* had only bunker capacity for coal for nine days' steaming. So wooden sailing ships with supplementary steam engines driving screw propellers still had much to commend them for fleet actions, convoying merchant craft and long distance passages.

At the same time as steam power was being introduced, naval gunnery was improving and rifled breech-loading shell guns were replacing the muzzle-loading cannon firing solid projectiles. Armour plating was being developed, but the thickest armour plating still proved inadequate in trials against the heavier explosive shells.

The answer, temporarily at least, was to combine the properties of iron and wood for greater protection. *La Gloire* achieved this with a wooden hull, encased in iron. The Admiralty's response was to go for a more radical approach – an iron hull encased in a teak cladding with an armour-plated central citadel. Eighteen inches of teak and 4¼ inches of armour plating protected the central area where the guns were mounted. The hull construction reflected the vast collective experience of British merchant ship designers and builders. John Scott Russell, who had advised the Admiralty on the *Warrior* class design had been intimately involved in the design of the gigantic *Great Eastern* and in the next slip to the *Black Prince* in Robert Napier's yard, work was going on to build the iron paddle steamer *Scotia* for the Cunard Company – destined to be the second largest merchant ship afloat, surpassed only by the *Great Eastern*.

The *Warrior* and *Black Prince* still mounted their main armament in a broadside along the main deck – the age of the turret ship had not yet arrived, although Captain Coles of the Royal Navy was advocating just such a design. The old, and somewhat unstable, triple gun deck of the *Victory* and her sister ships had been reduced to one main gun deck (hence the somewhat odd technical classification of *Black Prince* as a frigate, despite it being much larger than any of the contemporary battleships), albeit with guns firing a 68 pound ball compared to the 32, 24 and 12 pounder batteries on the three principal gun decks of the *Victory* at Trafalgar.

Black Prince's armament varied over her career but initially she was designed to mount 34 of those large 68 pounder muzzle-loading cannons on her main deck and added four lighter 40 pounders and two pivot guns firing a 100 pound projectile on an upper deck. These upper-deck guns were breech-loading Armstrong guns. In effect a similar broadside weight of shell could be achieved with fewer piercings in the side of the ship and, consequently, a higher level of resistance to enemy fire.

Although her engines produced 1,250 horsepower, capable of driving her at a speed of around 14 knots, she was still rigged in the same way as the old three-decker line of battle ships. Not until full rigging could be eliminated would it become practical to design ocean-going ships capable of long passages with central, turret-mounted guns. Earlier iron-clad ships, which had relied almost exclusively on steam power – including vessels such as the monitor *Erebus* built by Napier during the Crimean War – had been little more than floating batteries designed to attack Russian fortifications.

The contract for *Warrior* went to the Thames Iron Works and Shipyard, and the engines for both *Black Prince* and *Warrior* were manufactured by Penn at Greenwich on the Thames.

The contract to build *Black Prince* might have been a great vote of confidence in Napier and the Clyde but it proved to be something of a mixed blessing. His yard had to be extended to cope with the new ship, the Clyde had to be dredged to allow her to be launched, and in the event his costs outstripped the contract sum and *Black Prince* lost Napier around £35,000. She was also delivered late (as was *Warrior*), due in part to the Admiralty's habit of changing its mind about design and specification. Indeed, the contractual penalties for late delivery were not enforced, as the Secretary to the Admiralty explained to Parliament:

> … it was not thought advisable that the penalties should be imposed, especially on account of various alterations being necessary, and having by so much retarded the works.[1]

On 27 February 1861, a cold, wet and windy day, Robert Napier's granddaughter Lizzie, in front of a large crowd of spectators who lined

---

[1] Hansard (House of Commons) 11 July 1861

FIG. 8.1

HMS *Black Prince* photographed after her 1875 refit.

us Naval Historical Center

both banks of the river, launched the ship into the waters of the Clyde. *The Times* reporter noted the crowds and reflected that the launch of all the iron frigates ever built would not attract such crowds in London in such weather, but that the people of the Clyde seemed to have a different degree of interest and commitment:

> Everyone seemed to have a personal interest in what was about to take place, and to feel proud of the completion of the noble vessel and the additional renown it would bring to Clyde ships and ship-builders. This identification with the ships built on the river by the people of Glasgow and its neighbouring towns has been a notable feature of the Clyde down the years.

At 419 feet from bowsprit to taffrail, 58 feet in beam, *Black Prince* was, as the reporter for the *Glasgow Herald* commented, 'a singularly handsome and very sharp screw vessel'. She was, in fact, so large that only three docks – Portsmouth, Southampton and Liverpool – were able to accommodate her. A remarkable, if anachronistic, feature was her 16-foot high figurehead, depicting the Black Prince (the son of King Edward III of England) in his armour, carved by the Glasgow firm of Kay and Reid.

The *Herald* reporter gave a detailed description of her construction. The cladding of the iron hull in finest East Indies teak was carried out in two layers – an inner layer 10 inches thick running fore and aft, and an outer layer of eight inches running vertically. Over this was placed forged iron armour plates, each 4½ inches thick, which were fitted together with a tongue and groove arrangement. Many of these plates were made at the Parkhead Forge, Glasgow, a Napier subsidiary, managed by Robert Napier's son-in-law, William Rigby. In all, 900 tons of armour plate protected the central citadel where the main armament was located. The *Herald* report concluded with the pointed comment:

> We cannot but feel surprised that the Lords of the Admiralty should have denied Glasgow the privilege of constructing the machinery of the *Black Prince*, looking to the historical connection of the Clyde with the rise and development of steam navigation, and to the character which Glasgow maintains as inferior to none of the shipbuilding ports of the world.

The Times reporter commented that:

> Messrs Napier's yard alone could complete three vessels like the *Black Prince* in a year; and though that is, perhaps, one of the finest yards in the kingdom, it is not the only one on the Clyde equal to the rapid manufacture of these stupendous frigates.

It was just this rich resource of engineering, shipbuilding knowledge and industrial capacity that made it possible for the Admiralty to surpass the French in the number and quality of iron ships. Indeed it was the British technology base which enabled the Admiralty to go for iron construction rather than just iron cladding of wooden hulls – France could not produce sufficient iron of the requisite quality for the Imperial government's ambitious plans to be realised in iron hulls – hence her adoption of the less ambitious wooden construction of *La Gloire* and her consorts.

After her launch and final work carried out at Govan, *Black Prince* was taken down to Greenock to have her machinery put on board and the last of the armour plating applied. By July 1861 she was carrying out trial trips on the Clyde and in November arrived at Portsmouth for the considerable amount of work to be done to fit her for commissioning. This included a new rudder, determined to be necessary in the light of experience with HMS *Warrior*. Trials were carried out, which proved *Black Prince* to be about 1 knot slower than the supposedly identical *Warrior*. Whether this was due to subtle differences in construction, in damage caused by an accident while fitting out at Greenock, or to other reasons seems unclear.

Eventually, in the summer of 1862 she was commissioned under Captain J. F. B. Wainwright and joined the Channel Fleet. Her guns had already been changed, with eight Armstrong 100 pound rifled muzzle-loaders being installed on the main gun deck, four forward and four aft, and the 34 muzzle-loading unrifled 68 pounders reduced to 26.

In 1863 *Black Prince*, *Warrior* and another three iron-clads of the Channel Fleet paid a visit to Scottish waters and attracted great enthusiasm from the Scottish public. Anchoring at the Tail of the Bank, crowds of interested spectators visited *Black Prince* and her consorts, while Greenock Town Council entertained the Admiral and his officers at a grand ball.

After four years in the Channel Fleet, *Black Prince* re-commissioned as flagship of the Admiral Commanding the Coast of Ireland. In 1867 she was paid off and re-armed with 32 rifled muzzle-loaders in place of the mix of weapons she had previously carried. The next year she became a unit of the First Reserve and was posted as guard-ship to the Clyde. During this period she left the Clyde to take part, with her sister ship HMS *Warrior*, in towing a floating dock to the naval base at Ireland Island, Bermuda. In 1874 she was refitted with a flag officer's accommodation on the poop and in 1875 was commissioned as flagship of the flag-officer, second in command, Channel Fleet and bore the flag of Lord John Hay.

In 1878 she was again a 'private ship' – that is, not the ship of a flag-officer – and was the command of Captain HRH the Duke of Edinburgh, the second son of Queen Victoria. During this commission she was sent to Canada to take part in the ceremonies for the installation of the Marquis of Lorne as Governor General. The Marquess, heir to the Duke of Argyll, was brother-in-law to the Duke of Edinburgh through his marriage to Queen Victoria's daughter, Princess Louise.

After the Canadian voyage, *Black Prince* was paid off into the Fleet

Reserve. In 1896 she went to Queenstown (now Cobh), Ireland ,to serve as a recruit training ship, but there proved to be insufficient Irish recruits to justify a training centre and she returned to the UK, serving as an accommodation ship at Plymouth. Renamed *Emerald* in 1903 to free the name *Black Prince* for a Duke of Edinburgh class armoured cruiser which entered service in 1906, she was again renamed *Impregnable III* in 1910 and was scrapped in 1923.

Built to meet a threat which was always more apparent than real, *Black Prince* was significant as the first major Royal Navy warship built on the Clyde and, despite her mysterious lack of speed when compared to *Warrior*, she was seen as a handsome and impressive ship. One contemporary observer, Charles Dickens, wrote of the visually identical *Warrior*: 'as black, vicious, ugly customer as ever I saw, whale-like in size, and with as terrible a row of incisor teeth as ever closed on a French frigate', while Napoleon III, who, after all, had given birth to her through his building programme, perhaps ruefully described *Warrior* as 'a raven among the daws'.

Black Prince was a significant part of the Clyde's developing story as the great arsenal for the Navy. Napier's central role in this was, oddly enough, never recognised by his country, although other countries, including France, showered honours on him. He was made a Chevalier of the Legion of Honour by Napoleon III of France, and the King of Denmark, following his construction of the turret ship *Rolf Kraké* for the Danish Navy, created him a Knight Commander of the Dannebrog. A naval officer wrote to Napier to congratulate him on this distinction and observed:

> ... may our Queen be induced to show her appreciation of your valuable services to our Navy by conferring a similar honour in the shape of a K.C.B. Why not? for, as Jack says 'You builds 'em, we sails 'em'.[2]

---

2   Napier, James, *Life of Robert Napier*, William Blackwood, Edinburgh, 1904

CHAPTER 9

Cutty Sark (1869–)

*She was the sublimated essence of all the clipper ships
which had preceded her.*
C. Nepean Longridge[1]

THIS IS THE SPECIAL ONE. This is the acme of beauty, the quintessence of efficiency – the ultimate sailing ship. Perhaps one of 'the most nearly perfect creations ever made by man for man's service'; the finest example of the finest type of pure sailing craft; a 'witch' of the seas that represented the supreme achievement of the naval architecture of the day. And all of this at the same time, as it turned out, as the revolution in shipbuilding that accompanied the arrival of steam propulsion.

For all who knew her, or have seen her or representations of her, the *Cutty Sark* had that particularly satisfying kind of beauty which always belongs to an object or artefact absolutely fitted for the purpose it is designed to serve. Current ideas of the process of design technology and the search for 'fitness for purpose' could have matched exactly the development of the ships that were part of the last generation of cargo sailing vessels. Normally classified as clipper ships, they were admired by all who saw them; none more so than the Scots-built tea clipper, whose given name (the sobriquet of the comely fleet-footed witch from Robert Burns's 'Tam o' Shanter') stands out among the place names and VIPs' names and classical allusions – it is a name that has somehow helped to bestow on its bearer unrivalled fame and celebrity. Less revolutionary than the steamship, the *Cutty Sark* can be said to have appeared as the product of an evolutionary process, which is another way of saying 'sublimated essence'.

The designer in question was Hercules Linton, and the ship, his masterpiece, was launched into the River Leven at Dumbarton in 1869.

When British shipping companies began ordering US 'Yankee' clipper

[1] Longridge, C. Nepean, *The Cutty Sark, The Last of the Famous Tea Clippers*, Percival Marshall, London, 1958

ships for the China tea trade, Scotland's shipyards were spurred on to design their own clippers. The high prices obtained in London for the first of each season's tea crop led to races from China to Britain. For example, leaving Foochow between 29 and 31 May 1866, the *Fiery Cross, Ariel, Taeping, Taitsing* and *Serica* all reached London between 6 and 8 September; the *Serica* completed the 25,744 kilometre (16,000 mile) voyage in less than 100 days. This is one of the clipper races that the American poet, Hart Crane, evokes in his poem 'The Bridge', about the Brooklyn Bridge (1930):

> Blithe Yankee vanities, turreted sprites, winged
> British repartees, skil-
>
> ful savage sea-girls
> that bloomed in the spring – Heave, weave
> those bright designs the trade winds drive...
>
> > *Sweet opium and tea, Yo-ho!*
> > *Pennies for porpoises that bank the keel!*
> > *Fins whip the breeze around Japan!*
>
> Bright skysails ticketing the Line, wink round the Horn
> to Frisco, Melbourne...
> Pennants, parabolas –
> clipper dreams indelible and ranging,
> baronial white on lucky blue!
>
> Perennial-*Cutty*-trophied-*Sark*!
>
> *Thermopylae, Black Prince, Flying Cloud* through Sunda
> – scarfed of foam, their bellies veered green esplanades,
> locked in wind-humors, ran their eastings down;
>
> > *at Java Head freshened the nip*
> > *(sweet opium and tea!)*
> > *and turned and left us on the lee...*
>
> Buntlines tusseling (91 days, 20 hours and anchored!)
> *Rainbow, Leander*
>
> (last trip a tragedy) – where can you be
> *Nimbus?* and you rivals two –

a long tack keeping –

Taeping?
Ariel?[2]

As befits a ship named after a witch, *Cutty Sark* had uncertain beginnings. The shipbuilders Scott and Linton were responsible for the better part of her construction, but, perhaps because of Linton's and her first skipper Captain George Moodie's perfectionism regardless of cost, the company failed and the *Cutty Sark* was completed by the adjacent shipbuilding firm of Denny's of Dumbarton, after her launch on 25 November 1869, as the *Dumbarton Herald* had reported:

> On Monday afternoon there was launched from the shipbuilding yard of Messrs Scott & Linton, a handsome composite clipper ship of the following dimensions: Length, 210 feet; beam, 36 feet; depth of hold, 20 feet 9 inches, and about 950 tons burthen… the *Cutty Sark* is intended for the China tea trade, and is expected by her owners to be one of the fastest ships engaged in that traffic.[3]

A composite vessel refers to the ship's structure and selection of materials, in this case an iron framework supporting a wooden hull (including American rock elm) and was an illustration of the rapid advances in shipbuilding that were going on in the second half of the 19th century. The advantages of composite construction were:

- increased strength with decreased weight;
- enlarged cargo capacity;
- when sheathed in copper it offered increased resistance to bottom-fouling (a particular problem for ships operating in tropical waters).

This was a significant stage in the gradual move from timber to iron construction (and shortly afterwards, steel).

It was, of course, the Americans who pioneered the clipper ships. The 'Yankee' clippers (which owed something to the naval frigates) were fast and slender, with a narrow hull and sail-plans comprising many hundreds

---

[2] Hart Crane, Stephen, *The Bridge, Complete Poems and Selected Letters*, The Library of America, 2006
[3] The Tea Council of Great Britain. Quote from publicity pamphlet

of square yards of sails on masts, spars and rigging. Some had as many as six tiers of sails to a mast, and a total of 35 sails. The clippers' name came from the way that they 'clipped off' the miles. The first British tea clipper, *Stornoway*, was built in Aberdeen in 1850. Here is the graphic description of the early races given by the United Kingdom Tea Council:

> The time of the international races was relatively short lived though, because after 1855 the American ships gradually ceased to participate in the English tea trade. But even without the Anglo-American rivalry, the competitive spirit continued. It was really ignited in 1853, when new ports in China were opened up for trade. These included Fouchow, which was much closer to the tea producing areas than Canton, the port used previously. As a result the tea could be loaded onboard earlier and fresher, and the clippers could set off in late May or early June – sometimes not even taking time to complete the official paperwork – racing back to Britain come hell or high water. They thundered down through the South China Sea and into the Indian Ocean, then raced to round the southern-most tip of Africa at the Cape of Good Hope. Then it was north across the vast Atlantic, past the Azores, through the English Channel and into the Thames estuary, from where they would be towed down the Thames by tugs.

Until the advent of the clipper the run-of-the-mill sailing ship had been capable of speeds of seven or eight knots at best – now thoroughbreds like the Aberdonian *Thermopylae*, *Cutty Sark's* greatest rival, were managing speeds of up to 20 knots. What was it, then, that was distinctive about the Clyde-built masterpiece bearing the name taken from the Ayrshire poet's tour de force?

Linton was a man driven on, above all, by the need for speed. One of the main factors that determined speed in a sailing vessel (setting aside variables such as wind and tide) was the configuration of sails, rigging, masts and spars. As was regular practice on the Clyde, the *Cutty Sark's* initial sail-plan was carried out by a Greenock firm.

The Scots connection with the manufacture of sailcloth was, from the late 18th century, most evident on the east coast of the country. Arbroath was a primary centre for sailmaking from imported flax. The biggest firm was D. Corsar & Sons, with its huge bleachfields and sail lofts. Their world-famous product was called 'Reliance' sailcloth. This stuff was 'the best' and on some occasions at least *Cutty Sark* used 'Reliance'. It was said that 'every square inch of her sail pattern came from Arbroath' (the jute to make the sails, of course, came into the country via nearby Dundee). Further north on the coast, at Inverbervie, there is a memorial to Linton.

The *Cutty Sark*'s builder believed that another, perhaps most important design feature that had a bearing on speed through the water was the shape of the hull. Most designs favoured the deep keel-like v-shaped hull; however, Linton's vision was different – as rendered by Scott and Linton's chief draughtsman, John Rennie, Linton's design for the hull incorporated a longer bowl-shape that he calculated could carry more sail as well as being stronger and (with the sharpest of 'entrances') ultimately faster. When the ship model was finished, the designers and Lloyd's surveyors were concerned with the 'knife-like' entrance. They thought she had so much cutaway that she required more bearing forward and would therefore lack power. However, Linton was right; they were wrong. The bowl-like hull and powerful quarters counteracted the sharp bow, and the *Cutty Sark* proved herself to be a magnificent sea boat.

This was to be the way that the 'dream-clipper' as requested by Captain John 'Jock' Willis, the ship's first owner, would be delivered. As remembered by one of her apprentices in later years, her performance was staggering, especially in the teeth of strong gales and in the trade winds:

> She simply slid through the water, and we overhauled and passed every ship ahead of us, sometimes going past them as if they were at anchor.

In calmer conditions, which were supposed to be less favourable to the little clipper, even then, as reported by the same observer: 'Just the flap of her sails was enough to send her along'.

An interesting echo of present-day concerns about fossil fuel resources came in a comment made in 1948 by C. Fox Smith. Ships like the *Cutty Sark* were built, he wrote:

> … such as the world had never known before and – unless indeed something unforeseen should happen to its supplies of coal and oil fuel – will never know again.[4]

Well, could there be a sort of reincarnation of these wonderful ships in

---

[4] Smith, C. Fox, *The Return of the Cutty Sark*, Methuen, London 1925

FIG. 9.1
A pre-First World War photo of *Cutty Sark* lying at Falmouth.

Authors' Collection

the form of the white-sailed motorised cruise ships of our day, though without the same necessity to go aloft to take in sail in stormy weather?

To continue, however, with the *Cutty Sark*'s early career. At the time of her launch, in a sense her nemesis was already at hand. In that same edition of the *Dumbarton Herald* newspaper in 1869 it was reported, most significantly, that:

> On Tuesday there was launched by Messrs Wm. Denny & Brothers an iron screw steamship of 1200 tons, intended principally as a cargo steamer via Suez Canal to India. Machinery of 150 horse-power nominal, on direct-acting surface condensation principle, will be fitted up by Messrs Denny & Co.

Here there is a clear symbol of a quite different, more threatening kind of trading competition faced by clipper ships at the time of the *Cutty Sark*'s rather late entry on the stage. The context was the expansion in world trade in a period relatively free of international conflicts and experiencing a contemporary boom in shipbuilding. Since the day of Bell's *Comet*, steam-powered ships (the despised 'steam-kettles') had gradually developed and now began to eat into the trading routes previously dominated by the aristocrats of sail. Two things may have finally tipped the balance against the tea and wool clippers and other fleet-footed vessels under canvas. One was something also alluded to in the *Herald* report – the opening of the Suez Canal in that same year of 1869 meant considerable savings in fuel and time for voyages to and from the East and the Antipodes. The other was the invention by A. C. Kirk in 1876 of the more efficient triple expansion engine, which eventually developed greater speed and power than the lovely sailing clippers. Ships could now conquer time and distance in a way never possible before. As Joseph Conrad, that great Polish author turned 'honorary' Scotsman, put it in *The End of the Tether*:

> Departed the opportunities… and gone with them the white-winged flock of clippers that lived in the boisterous uncertain life of the winds, skimming big fortunes out of the foam of the sea. [The] ships now had yellow funnels with black tops, and a time-table of appointed routes like a confounded service of tramways.[5]

---

[5] Conrad, Joseph, *The End of the Tether*, J.M. Dent and Sons, London, 1946

First though, the little Clyde-built *Cutty Sark* was to have her moments of glory – it was time, as Burns wrote of her original:

> To sing how Nannie lap and flang,
> A souple jade she was and strang.

Scott and Linton designed the *Cutty Sark* specifically for the China Tea Trade Race, an amazing sort of unofficial competition – followed assiduously by thousands of enthusiasts – among the shipping companies for the fastest delivery to Europe, via the Cape of Good Hope, of the new crop of the coveted China tea. That involved loading up at Shanghai and other ports, and by way of the Cape the rival fleets of clippers would vie with each other to make the fastest time to the London Docks. Loading the tea required the greatest degree of skill and ingenuity. The tea chests needed to be packed incredibly tightly, not simply to maximise the cargo, but also to prevent it shifting when the ship was under way. Fear of a cargo shifting was a constant concern, since the vessel could easily be thrown off balance and in serious cases might founder. The Chinese stevedores packed the chests in tiers, sometimes hammering them into place with great wooden mallets. It was skilled work carried out at great speed, and equally skilled were the dockers whose job it was to unload the cargo at the other end of the homeward passage.

In the event the *Cutty Sark* had a relatively brief encounter with the China Trade, but she had a longer and on the whole more memorable series of voyages from Australia and for the wool trade. To concentrate on Captain Moodie's famous tea race with the *Thermopylae* in 1872 for the moment, this contest falls, fortunately, in the period covered by the surviving logbooks of the *Cutty Sark*. There are accounts of the race in various histories and newspapers but Dumbarton Library is fortunate to have abstracts of logs (with mainly non-navigational information) donated by Captain Moodie late in life, and these would seem to provide more reliable information about the first exciting encounter with *Thermopylae*. According to the log Moodie sighted the *Thermopylae* on the 15, 17, 18 and 20 July 1872, the last date at a position off the north-west coast of Australia, near Christmas Island. So, at this stage in the race they were neck and neck; nevertheless, as is well known and many yarns or seamen's baurs relate, the *Cutty Sark* did not 'win' that first epic race. She finally came into British waters less than a week after her rival – having been 600–800 miles ahead of *Thermopylae*, until her celebrated misfortune with the smashed rudder. This damage was incurred near Cape Town in circumstances that can perhaps be imagined from the following entries in the log:

1872

13 August	*Blowing a very heavy gale. Main and Fore Lower Topsails went to pieces. Hard gale continues... tremendous sea.*
15 August	*Hard gale, at 6.30 heavy sea struck rudder and knocked it away... (later) tried spar over the stern, but would not steer the ship.*
17 August	*Constructing jury rudder and sternpost as fast as possible...*
2 September (following more gales)	*Steers very well with wind right aft, but with a stiff side wind she steers very indifferently.*[6]

A handful more years on the tea trade followed, with no further meetings with speedy rivals, and after 1877 she carried no more cargoes of the much-sought after China tea.

Next, she had a period spent carrying mixed cargoes, such as coal and jute, where the *Cutty Sark* had no particular necessity or opportunity to show her sheer speed. There were a number of somewhat lurid incidents involving her crew, however, including several bouts of drinking mingled with prayer meetings, a master who went to feed the sharks in the Java Sea, and various tales surrounding two successive skippers called, appropriately enough, Wallace and Bruce.

In 1885 Captain R. Woodget took over for a considerable number of voyages, for the most part carrying wool from Sydney, and wool proved to be a suitable cargo for Woodget's new command – Woodget's crew proved particularly adept at loading or 'screwing in' the bales to every possible nook and cranny of the hold. With tea the objective of the clippers was to be first home with precious tea. With wool the aim was to be home in time to catch the January and February wool sales. In this case the slower ships departed first with the fastest clippers remaining in Australia to seize the later sheep-shearings and then make a break for home. It was during this period that the *Cutty Sark* really put paid to her rivals, notably

---

[6] Copy of log of the *Cutty Sark* in West Dunbartonshire Council Archive

Thermopylae. Woodget's first run with the Dumbarton-built clipper on the wool passages was in 1885. She left Sydney loaded with 4,465 bales of wool from New South Wales on 16 October and reached the Downs on December 28 after a passage of 73 days. These were heady days – Conrad wrote of:

> Those iron wool-clippers that the Clyde had floated out in swarms upon the world during the seventh decade of the (19th) century. It was a fine period in ship-building...[7]

The 'wool races' took place from autumn to spring and over the next 10 years a whole series of fast times from Australia to home, some as low as 60 odd days, were logged by the *Cutty Sark*. Her best run, of 360 nautical miles in 24 hours, was said to have been the fastest of any ship of her size.

So, the reign of the tea clippers was as brief as it was glorious. As has been mentioned, in November 1869 the Suez Canal opened, creating a navigable passage between the Far East and the Mediterranean. Immediately, it became economically viable for steamships to ply the China tea trade. Until then, the amount of bunker coal the steamships needed to carry to complete the journey to and from China, going by way of the Cape, left little room for the tea – a relatively bulky cargo. But going via the Suez Canal, the journey length was cut dramatically and the steamships became a more realistic alternative to the clippers, which could not use the Canal. The steamships never succeeded in appealing to the man in the street in the way that the immensely attractive clippers and their real or fictional crews had done. Not until the days of Conrad and *Lord Jim* did the master mariners, fictional and non-fictional, of the steamships begin to attract the same aura of glamour and hero worship as did those who crewed the 'dream-clippers'.

In 1895 Willis sold the *Cutty Sark* to the Portuguese firm of Ferreira, who renamed her after the firm, then in 1916 she was dismasted off the Cape of Good Hope, sold, re-rigged in Cape Town as a barquentine, and renamed the *Maria do Amparo*. In 1922 she was bought by Captain Wilfred Dowman, who restored her to her original appearance and used her as a stationary training ship. In 1954 she was dry-docked at Greenwich.

The *Cutty Sark* is today preserved as a museum ship, and is a popular tourist attraction at Greenwich on the Thames, beside the National

---

[7] Conrad, Joseph, *A Personal Record*, J.M. Dent & Sons, London, 1912

Maritime Museum and the splendid Greenwich Hospital and Park. Kept in a dry dock since 1954, the *Cutty Sark* has deteriorated considerably. As the Cutty Sark Trust points out:

> In 1869, when *Cutty Sark* was launched, the ship was expected to have a life of around 30 years. *Cutty Sark* has lasted 4½ times longer. Her 135-year history has been one of continual repairs, refits, maintenance, and ultimately restoration. Yet she still retains around 90–95% of the hull fabric that served her during her sea-going career, and this fabric continues to survive without significant loss of strength or integrity.

The Trust was forced to close her to the public in 2007 to allow for a complete renovation and the construction of new visitor facilities. An application for funding was made to the Heritage Lottery Fund and £13 million was granted. Work commenced in 2006 on an ambitious plan to conserve the hull and preserve the *Cutty Sark* for future generations; it was planned to re-open the ship to the public in 2008. However:

> A gigantic flame arose forward straight and clear. It flared fierce, with noises like the whirr of wings, with rumbles as of thunder. There were cracks, detonations, and from the cone of flame the sparks flew upwards, as man is born to trouble, to leaky ships, and to ships that burn.[8]

This passage describing a fire on board a sailing vessel taken from *Youth* by Joseph Conrad might have sprung to mind on 21 May 2007, when the Cutty Sark burned at the dry dock in Greenwich and sent a flame of shock and horror round the world to wherever there is respect and affection for a maritime heritage. Who could have predicted that a clipper built in a small Dumbarton shipyard would have been the lead story in international news bulletins? In the few weeks since the disaster there have been many eloquent expressions of concern and support. Libby Purves enthuses:

> … You cannot walk the wide decks or creep the narrow passages of an old ship without imagining how it would be when it lurched and creaked and plunged, week after week, the only man-made object for a thousand miles… We have a wonderfully vivid ship-shaped history.[9]

---

[8] Conrad, Joseph, *Youth*, J.M. Dent & Sons, London, 1902
[9] *The Times*, 2007

No one is yet clear about the chances of restoration, nor even of 'saving' the 138-year-old vessel. Many hazards will arise when the rescuers come to deal with *Cutty Sark*'s almost unique composite structure – in particular, the iron framework presents problems, if it has been seriously warped in the heat. On the other hand, the fact that vital components like the masts were placed in safe store while the planned restoration work was going on is just one positive factor. Most lovers of the comely witch, and there are many, are optimists. To paraphrase Purves – The *Cutty Sark* may still have a ship-shaped future.

CHAPTER 10

Glenlee and Other Clyde Veterans (1896–)

TWENTY-SEVEN YEARS after the launch of Scotland's greatest sailing vessel, the *Cutty Sark*, yet another Clyde-built sailing ship, destined to be rescued, restored and preserved in our own day, slipped fully rigged into the waters of the River Clyde. The *Glenlee* was a three-masted steel-built barque, built by A. Rodger & Company at Port Glasgow. Of 1,613 gross tonnage she had a length of 233.3 feet, beam of 37.5 feet and draught of 22.5 feet. In 1992, when she was bought by Dr Hamish Hardie, she lay:

> A hulk half full of water, stripped of her masts, her brasswork stolen, vandalised and derelict in a remote part of Seville harbour.[1]

By July 1999 her restoration was complete and *Glenlee* made an acclaimed public appearance at the Tall Ships Festival on the Clyde, less than a mile from the place of her launch a century before. According to the Clyde Maritime Trust's account of the rescue programme, the *Glenlee* is barque-rigged with identical fore and main masts. The topgallant masts and upper topgallant yards were originally made of pitch pine and the rest of riveted steel sections that were later welded. When the masts and rigging were re-assembled during the restoration work in the 1990s, it was found convenient to replace the welded sections with steel riveted masts and yards.

    Glenlee was destined to have a chequered career, flying the red ensign under several owners until 1921, when she embarked on a long career as a Spanish training ship, partly during the monarchy and partly during the period of Franco's fascist dictatorship. The Spaniards called her *Galatea*, and she collected a number of other names in her long voyage across the world's oceans. These 30 years from her launch was a period when the role of sailing ships changed irrevocably, from ships that were

[1] Ed. Clyde Navigation Trust and Dr Hamish Hardie, *The Dutchman had Guilders, the story of the Glenlee*, 2003

thoroughbreds to workhorses of limited range, widely seen as inferior to the all-conquering steam power. The supreme novelist of maritime matters, Joseph Conrad, wrote in *The Mirror of the Sea* (1906):

> The modern steamship advances upon a still and overshadowed sea with a pulsating tremor of her frame, an occasional clang in her depths, as if she had an iron heart in her iron body; with a thudding rhythm in her progress and the regular beat of her propeller, heard afar in the night with an august and plodding sound as of the march of an inevitable future.[2]

Conrad was conceding that, in a way, he had glimpsed 'Historical Inevitability' on the horizon. Others in the Scottish shipping world had earlier felt the same. In 1869, in the same week as the finest of all clipper ships, Scott & Linton's *Cutty Sark* was launched, Denny of Dumbarton, the Dumbarton shipbuilder who was to complete her, also launched an iron sailing ship, called *Invereshie*, for Messrs J. & S. Grant. The *Invereshie* was, according to the *Dumbarton Herald*:

> intended to form one of their East India fleet, and has, with a view to going through the Suez Canal, provision for auxiliary steam power.

This is evidence that smart operators were hedging their bets, or using strategic thinking in the fiercely competitive world of the shipping lines. In the very year that the Suez Canal was opened to traffic, the message was that the balance was tipped for steam over sail, particularly in Far East voyages.

Nevertheless, the sailing ship had shown a remarkable resilience in the face of the new technology, and still clung to an important role in the world shipping scene, even into the 20th century. Statistics show that, in 1905, there were still 1,537 United Kingdom registered sailing ships of 100 tons and above on Lloyd's Register of Shipping – there were 10,823 sailing ships worldwide. Just as amazing is the fact that in that year 31.5% of total world shipping was UK registered. Scots often emphasise the percentage of world shipping built on the Clyde, but really just as significant is the grip the UK had on world shipping. Around one in three of the ships of the world flew the Red Ensign – a huge amount of the international

---

[2] Conrad, Joseph, *Mirror of the Sea*, J.M. Dent & Sons, London, 1906

FIG. 10.1
Glenlee's bell
Authors' Collection

trade of third parties must have been carried in British ships. Invisible exports: shipping, insurance and financial services, helped to keep Britain prosperous even when the US, Germany and Japan overtook British industrial production; in steam ships the UK registry was 41.6% of the world total.

Many were like Conrad in preferring the old ways of sail rather than steam – or possibly a combination of the two. His challenging response to the steamship's threatening march towards the 'inevitable future' was essentially a Romantic one:

> (But) in a gale, the silent machinery of a sailing-ship would catch not only the power, but the wild and exulting voice of the world's soul.

Of course the author of *Heart of Darkness* served on a number of Clyde-built ships and would have recognised the *Glenlee* type as playing a familiar but substantial role in world trade. In the year of the completion of the Port Glasgow-built *Glenlee* there were 936 iron-hulled sailing ships under UK registration and 515 of the more innovative type steel hulls. *Glenlee*, the name she once again bears as she lies at Glasgow Quay in the upper part of the river that gave her birth, is a typical mixed cargo-carrying merchant ship of the late Victorian period. She has a steel frame with overlapping steel plates riveted on to frames 2 feet apart. She is conventionally barque rigged with her lower masts, topmasts and topgallants made of steel originally riveted and then in later years welded. All these features can be seen at the 'Tall Ship', where the masts and spars of the *Glenlee* tower above the Clydeside Expressway and the 'permanent way' of the northbank rail services.

In the First World War, at that juncture with the name *Islamount*, she was owned by a group of shareholders who hailed predominantly from Dundee. More exotically, from 1921 she served as a training or school ship for the Spanish Navy and made two or three training cruises every year. *Galatea* had been re-configured to carry around 250 cadets, and maintained a busy schedule right up to 1969, when her sea service came to an end. *Glenlee/Galatea* now faced the most inglorious part of her career. Other ideas having failed to bear fruit, she was towed to Seville Harbour on Spain's Guadalquivir River and allowed to quietly rot away, with nothing in view save for the breakers' yard. She remained at Seville

FIG. 10.2
Glenlee's figurehead
Authors' Collection

until a group of enthusiasts based in Glasgow mounted their own rescue operation in 1992, some four years short of the old lady's first century – the Clyde Maritime Trust rescued the vessel they re-christened *Glenlee* and after an epic voyage brought her to the Clyde.

A handful of other Clyde-built sailing ships besides the *Glenlee* survive and form a sort of elite sisterhood. For example, the *Balclutha* was built in 1886 by Charles Connell & Co. Ltd., of Glasgow, for Robert McMillan of

Dumbarton. Balclutha was a name selected by someone who knew their history – the name means 'rock' or 'town' on the Clyde (more often rendered as 'Alcluith') and can be identified with Dumbarton Rock and its archaeological remains. As such, Balclutha appears in the *Poems of Ossian*, by James Macpherson:

> I have seen the walls of Balclutha, but they were desolate. The fire had resounded in the halls: and the voice of the people is heard no more.[3]

As things turned out, the career of *Balclutha* the ship was more than once almost as 'desolate' as Balclutha the place, in the poem 'Carthon'. However, the ship has come to a happy end, in no less a place than San Francisco.

Designed as a general trader, *Balclutha* rounded Cape Horn 17 times in 13 years under various commands. During this period she carried cargoes such as wine, case oil, and coal from Europe and the east coast of the United States to various ports in the Pacific. These included Chile for nitrate, Australia and New Zealand for wool, Burma for rice, San Francisco for grain, and the Pacific Northwest for timber. In 1899 the *Balclutha* transferred to the registry of Hawaii, and traded timber from the Pacific Northeast to Australia, returning to San Francisco with Australian coal. She was a workaday ship in many respects but could show a clean pair of heels when required, as when she covered 68 sea miles in a four hour watch in 1906.

In 1902 the *Balclutha* was renamed the *Star of Alaska* and joined the salmon fishing trade, sailing north from the San Francisco area to Alaska in April with supplies, fishermen and cannery workers, and returned in September with canned salmon. For this trade she carried over 200 crew, as compared to the 26 man crew she carried as the *Balclutha*. Her last voyage in this trade was in 1930.

In 1933 the *Star of Alaska* was yet again renamed the *Pacific Queen*. Under this name she appeared in various Hollywood movies, including *Mutiny on the Bounty*, starring Clark Gable and Charles Laughton. In 1954 the *Pacific Queen* was acquired by the San Francisco Maritime Museum, who restored her and renamed her *Balclutha*. In 1985 she was designated a National Historic Landmark. She had a lengthy spell as an exhibition ship and is now one of the exhibits of the San Francisco

---

[3] MacPherson, James, *The Poems of Ossian*, edited by Howard Gaskill, Edinburgh University Press, 1996

Maritime National Historical Park and is to be found moored at the Park's Hyde Street Pier.

Balclutha

- Gross tonnage   1,689 tons   (1,716 tonnes)
- Overall length   301 feet   (91.7 metres)
- Length of deck   256.5 feet   (78.1 metres)
- Draught   22.7 feet   (6.92 metres)
- Beam   38.6 feet   (11.8 metres)

Another Clyde veteran is the *Falls of Clyde,* the only surviving iron-hulled, four-masted full rigged sailing vessel, and the only surviving sail-driven oil tanker in the world. She was built in 1878 by Russell and Company in Port Glasgow, launched as the first of eight iron-hulled four-masted barques built for Wright and Breakenridge's Falls Line. Her statistics are as follows: length 266 feet; beam 40 feet; draught 21 feet. The first six years of her career were spent on the India run. She then carried general cargo such as lumber, jute, cement, and wheat from ports in Australia, California, India, New Zealand and the UK.

After 21 years under the Red Ensign, the *Falls of Clyde* was purchased for US $25,000 by Captain Matson of the Matson Navigation Company, taken to Honolulu in 1899, and registered under the Hawaiian flag. When the Republic of Hawaii was annexed by the United States in 1900, it took a special act of the United States Congress to secure the foreign-built ship the right to fly the Stars and Stripes.

From 1899 to 1907, she made over 60 voyages between Hawaii and San Francisco, California. She carried general merchandise from San Francisco and sugar from Hawaii, and also a complement of passengers in both directions. She developed a reputation as a fast and commodious vessel; her voyages averaged 17 days each way.

In 1907, the Associated Oil Company bought the *Falls of Clyde* and converted her to a bulk tanker with a capacity of 19,000 barrels (3 million litres, 800,000 gallons). In this configuration she sailed from California, with kerosene, which she discharged in Honolulu at Pier 16. On her return voyages, she carried bulk molasses to California, where it was used for cattle feed.

In 1927 the barque was sold to the General Petroleum Company, her masts were cut down and she served as a floating fuel depot in Alaska until 1959. She was sold to William Mitchell, who towed her to Seattle, intending to sell her to a preservation group but without success. Subsequent efforts by the San Francisco Maritime Museum to place her in Long Beach or Los Angeles, were similarly disappointed. In 1963 the bank holding the mortgage on the *Falls of Clyde* decided to sell her, and she was to be sunk as part of a breakwater at Vancouver, British Columbia. Some activists aroused interest in the ship among sympathetic enthusiasts back in Hawaii, and within days of the planned scuttling of the old ship, raised sufficient funds to buy her. At the end of October 1963, *Falls of Clyde* was taken under tow by a US tug and taken to the Bishop Maritime Museum in Honolulu; after refitting she was opened to the public in 1968.

Falls of Clyde's restoration as a full-rigged ship was thorough and the work was, happily enough, overseen by the grandson of the original Scottish 19th-century designer, William Lithgow. This support came from the current William Lithgow, the shipbuilder and industrialist, whose Port Glasgow shipyard donated masts and other fittings. In 1973 she was entered into the US National Register of Historic Places. As recently as 2005, *Falls of Clyde* was located at Pier 7, in Honolulu Harbor, an important focal point of the Hawaii Maritime Center.

The final Port Glasgow-built survivor of turn of the century historical sailing ships, the steel four-masted barque *Moshulu*, following her launch as the *Kurt* at William Hamilton's yard in 1904, had a lengthy career sailing under various flags, including the German and the US. She had exceptionally large dimensions: length 335 feet; beam 46 feet; draught 26 feet. *Moshulu*, 100 feet longer than *Glenlee*, is now a floating restaurant at Penn's Landing, Philadelphia. As an authentic backdrop and precious survivor of an almost vanished maritime age, this old ship has also made appearances in various Hollywood movies, including *Rocky* and *The Godfather Part II*.

Moshulu, moored on the eastern seaboard of the United States, is one of a small group of historically significant Scottish-built ships scattered around the globe that have survived and are now open to tourists and lovers of historic ships alike.

CHAPTER 11

RRS *Discovery* and *Scotia* (1896–)

MIDWINTER 1903: two ships, both built on whaling lines and with strong Scottish connections, are held fast in the ice of the Antarctic Ocean. One, frozen at anchor in the channel known as McMurdo Sound is the *Discovery*, the floating headquarters of the British National Antarctic Expedition, led by Captain Robert Falcon Scott. *Discovery* flies the White Ensign and the Union Jack. The other ship is almost a mirror image on the far side of the vast disc of the Southern Continent. Close to the recently discovered Weddell Sea, and also ice-bound, she flies the Saltire, and for good measure, the Lion Rampant. Proudly bearing the name *Scotia*, she carries the Scottish National Antarctic Expedition led by William Spiers Bruce. Both ships are caught in the winter pack-ice that surrounds the largely unexplored and uncharted islands, coast and land mass of Antarctica. They winter in the worst weather conditions on the planet.

The South Polar Region is also dotted with several other expeditions of European and other powers: Sweden, Germany and Argentina all have vessels busy with mapping, recording and other scientific work, at the same time as the *Discovery* and *Scotia* are engaged in their missions. To us today, all this activity bears a certain resemblance to the early years of manned space flight – the Space Race. At this stage in 1903, when the *Discovery* and others are tentatively exploring the Antarctic coast, they are, so to speak, trying to achieve moon orbit. The grand design is to be first to reach the South Pole, or achieve the equivalent to a moon landing.

From a Scottish point of view, what was remarkable about all this polar activity was the close involvement of Dundee, whaling port and ship-building centre, in the widespread craze at the beginning of the 20th century for exploring the Southern Continent. The age had an appetite for 'discovery' that preoccupied scientists and would-be scientists, explorers and naturalists – and even extended to the man reading his newspaper back home on the Clapham omnibus. *Discovery*, Scott's command ship on the dramatic and largely successful 1901 expedition, was built in Dundee. For a long time the shipbuilding industry in that city had been associated with the construction of whaling ships, some of which were capable of remaining at sea for years at a time (the record was the 11-year trip of an American whaler). Whalers, having exhausted vast stocks of whales in the Northern Atlantic and Arctic, were now venturing far into the Southern Ocean and proved adaptable for coping with the extreme conditions found there, so it was hardly surprising that when the Royal Societies were placing an order for a custom-built exploration/scientific research vessel they selected a design that owed much to the best features of whaling vessels; namely strength and, appropriately enough, endurance. (*Scotia* was a rebuilt Norwegian whaler known previously as *Hekla*.)

Other features of Antarctic exploration were also influenced by or modelled on recent experience in the Arctic Far North, the original Ultima Thule. The truth is that the maritime dimension in Antarctica was not the primary consideration as in the Arctic Sea ice-pack of the North Pole. This was something quite different – the immense, mountainous hostile continent of Antarctica demanded a different range of techniques and technologies of exploration. Even so, both north and south poles still excited in 1903 a particular focus for expeditions. Indeed, the North Pole was not actually conquered until Admiral Peary reached it in 1909, and the first vessel to reach the Pole (under the ice-cap) and surface there was the nuclear submarine USS *Skate*, exactly 50 years later. Scott was very much focused on the South Pole, Shackleton less so. Shackleton was to have his own considerable moment of fame with his ship *Endurance* and the epic journey to Elephant Island. The Scot, William Spiers Bruce, was quite different; more than the others, he deserved the term conservationist; he also found a surprising new role for a little Ayrshire seaside town:

> This is a voyage of discovery and scientific research – from Troon to the South Polar Regions...[1]

Scott and Bruce's expeditions and methodologies have left quite different legacies of fame, as have the men's personalities. The 1903 expeditions that found them trapped together in the southern ice are summarised

---

[1] Bruce, William Spiers, quoted in *William Spiers Bruce, Polar Explorer and Scottish Nationalist*, by Peter Speak, Edinburgh NMS Publishing, 2003

FIG. 11.1
Discovery
The veteran of Antarctic exploration preserved in the city where she was built.
Visit Scotland Angus & Dundee

below. Although Scott and Bruce had some shared aims that included, for example, scientific discovery, as well as what might be called ambition or individual and collective heroism, their actual achievements differed. Various statements of intent made by them illustrate how unalike their intentions were. In 1910, for example, Scott was still reacting to others' plans for exploration with this claim:

> The main object of this expedition is to reach the South Pole, to secure for the British Empire the honour of this achievement.

In contrast, in 1902 Bruce had written, obviously with others' publicity-seeking in mind:

> To reach the North Pole or South Pole is an athletic feat... It is not serious scientific work. We have already done biological work... we have made holes in the ice in various places and let down traps. These are visited every other day.

His friend Patrick Geddes, the contemporary Scots environmental guru, commented that Bruce's emphasis on science in his exploration was 'unparalleled in its completeness and range', unlike 'more dramatic expeditions'.

EXPLORERS AND SHIPS
Scott and *Discovery*

MAIN PURPOSE	The importance of the 'Race to the Pole' was implicit in all the expedition's work. Scott's personal ambition was an important factor. Publicity (and posterity) presented Scott as heroic figure. Success of this mission led to the tragic finale of his second expedition.
THE SHIP	*Discovery*, launched 21 March 1901 by Dundee Shipbuilders. Last UK wooden three-masted ship. Coal bunkers inadequate, so she was rigged as a barque and sailed to the Antarctic.
VOYAGE 1	Left Isle of Wight 6 Aug 1901. Jan 1902 charted some of coastline Feb 1902 anchors in McMurdo Sound. Becomes stuck fast in pack ice for two years. Ship used as a base most of time. Some cross-continent exploration carried out. (*Scotia* arrives in Weddell Sea on other side of the land-mass around this time.)

VOYAGE 2	Rescue mission by two other ships – one, the *Terra Nova*, used explosives to assist the gradual break-up of ice pack, 16 Feb 1904
RETURN TO UK	Return to Spithead, 10 Sep 1904. Ballyhoo ensued comparable to 21st-century kind. Scott's second expedition of 1910 used the *Terra Nova*.

Bruce and *Scotia*

MAIN PURPOSE	Bruce stressed the primacy of scientific survey and ecological matters. Very much in the tradition of Scots exploration and motives, e.g. Livingstone and Africa. Bruce had previously been involved in 11 expeditions to the Arctic and took part in the 1890–2 Dundee Whaling Expedition to the Antarctic. Two more expeditions to polar regions were to follow.
THE SHIP	*Scotia*, formerly a Norwegian whaler named *Hekla*. Converted to barque-rigged auxiliary screw steamer by Ailsa Shipbuilding Co. at Troon. Selected by Bruce to be similar to the Norwegian Nansen's *Fram*. *Hekla* had also been previously sailed by a Norwegian explorer.
VOYAGE 1	Left Troon in Ayrshire, 2 Nov 1902. Re-fit had delayed start and lost much of Antarctic summer. Called at Dublin for Guinness, from one of expedition's sponsors. Called at Falklands (6 Jan 1903) and S. Orkney Islands and crossed the Antarctic Circle into Weddell Sea. Onset of winter ice, so returned along edge of pack to S. Orkney Islands and Laurie Island, 21 Mar 1903. Ship ice-locked in Scotia Bay during winter of 1903.
VOYAGE 2	Thawing of sea ice on 27 Nov 1903. *Scotia* to Argentina for re-fit. Return to explore Weddell Sea. Naming of Coats Land after Coats of Paisley, expedition's main sponsor.
RETURN TO UK	Returned via Cape Town. Reached the Clyde for a grand reception at the Marine Station, Millport, on 21 July 1904.

The *Discovery* was the first ship to be specifically designed and built for scientific work. Her specification circulated to the press included the following clear but slightly conservative requirements:

> The ship will be 172 feet long, 33 feet extreme beam and will be 1,570 tons displacement. She will be built of oak and elm, with an ice casing of green heart. Her bows will be sharp and strengthened for forcing her way through ice. The plans are those of a vessel which will be, by far, the best adapted for severe weather and ice navigation, as well as for scientific investigations, that has ever entered the Polar Regions. She has to be a wooden ship to withstand the pressure of the ice [it was thought that steel would buckle from the immense pressure of the ice]. She has to be a sailing ship but with auxiliary engines – however the engines will be used sparingly because she cannot carry sufficient fuel.

The *Discovery* has retained her fame down the years, even though she only figured in Scott's (largely successful) first expedition. Her supplies included stores of oil, coal, fresh water and dog food. Contrary to the common belief that Scott did not favour the use of dog sleds, there were actually 25 Siberian dogs on board; it was simply that they were used sparingly, unlike those of Amundsen, the ultimate conqueror of the Pole. Medical supplies, scientific instruments, tools, a library and even a piano were listed. Not all of the planning and predictions about the expedition's needs and performance made at the time of building were accurate or well founded, as can be seen when we consider how realistic were the expectations expressed in *The Scotsman* newspaper report on the trial trip of the ship on 15 May 1901:

- When the *Discovery* leaves the region of civilisation and of coal depots, she will, however, make her own way mostly by means of canvas.

- In many departments of the expedition steam will be a valuable adjunct, particularly in the manoeuvring of the vessel to within a short distance of ice or shore… Its help in making way through a thin streak of ice, or backing out of an impossible 'bay' will be of importance to the navigators – a process which with sailing ships is commonly pursued in Polar Regions by laboriously 'warping' the vessel – i.e. by hauling on a rope or ropes secured to a fixed position. [In the event,

Discovery was to be trapped in the ice through two long winters, and she could not be moved until two rescue ships arrived, together with a significant thaw.]

- Electricity may be regarded as more or less of a luxury, but, to save consumption of coal... the dynamo has the assistance of an old-fashioned power in a windmill situated on the forecastle, and which can be transhipped on shore or iceberg as occasion demands.

Scott's ship made good progress down through the Atlantic and on to Antarctica. The general optimism of this first expedition (spent for the most part at the vast inlet of McMurdo Sound) was, of course, eventually to give way to the despair that he recorded in his diary at the Pole, when he wrote, 'This is an awful place'. After arriving at what they thought would be their winter quarters, the ship was secured by ice-anchors to a glacier foot and a square hut was built. Two smaller huts were put up to house the magnetic instruments and the dogs were moved into their kennels. On 16 February 1902, the sun dipped below the horizon for the first time. It was too late in the season for any long-distance sledge trips so Scott planned a few short practice trips to test the equipment and men. That same month the ice gripped and held *Discovery* so firmly that it would be two long seven-month winters before she could be freed, and the task of exploring and 'defining' this vast blank of a continent became all the more arduous.

During the two years that the ship remained locked in the ice, attempts to move overland towards the Pole were hampered by the conditions at McMurdo Sound, although other valuable, though less glamorous, discoveries were made during that seemingly never-ending period. On 27 January 1904 Scott wrote, 'I fear, I much fear, things are going badly for us.' Then, in February 1904, a definite thaw was noticed, there was enormous relief and an all-out attack on the ice was put into gear. Explosives, saws and everything imaginable were used in an attempt to free *Discovery*. On 12 February, another expedition member wrote, 'The *Terra Nova* [one of the rescue ships] is now only about two miles away and the ice continues to break away.' The ice was breaking up into huge lumps and floes. They worked feverishly to open up leads between the floes as the fate of the ship and the expedition hung in the balance. Two days later and the break they needed came as Scott saw from a vantage point that 'the ice was breaking-up right across the strait.' The relief ships broke through the ice-pack to the *Discovery*. The crew cheered as the *Terra Nova* cleared the last ice-ridge at 10.30pm and freed the expedition ship.

The Scottish National Antarctic Expedition was very much the product of its driving force, William Speirs Bruce (1867–1921), and was designed to increase scientific knowledge of the Antarctic Polar Regions. Unlike the *Discovery* Expedition, there was no intention of undertaking a major programme of exploration of the land mass. The *Scotia* skirted the southern continent's coastline and carried out much valuable scientific work there and in the South Orkney Islands and the Weddell Sea. The expedition sighted undiscovered land and this was named 'Coats Land' after the principal private patrons of the expedition, the Coats Brothers – textile manufacturers from Paisley, who had donated two thirds of the entire costs of the journey. After a period when the ship was caught in the ice pack, the *Scotia* was eventually 'liberated', in Bruce's words, and returned to Scotland on 21 July 1904.

On his return home in September of the same year, Captain Scott was feted everywhere. On 7 November he gave his first big lecture to 7,000 at the Albert Hall. He was awarded the Gold Medal of the Royal Geographical Society, made a member of the French Legion of Honour and the Russian Geographical Society, and received medals from other geographical societies, including those of Denmark and Sweden. By contrast, Bruce's voyage went almost unnoticed south of the border, despite much important scientific work and significant geographical discoveries. *Scotia* was sold (where else?) in Dundee to help to pay for the significant losses of the expedition. Her career as a whaler was resumed, but she later also worked as an observer-vessel on the North Atlantic Iceberg Patrol, following the *Titanic* disaster. *Scotia*'s end came during the First World War, when she caught fire and burned out on the Welsh coast.

Meanwhile, supporters pleaded with the government to retain the *Discovery* for future Polar work, but their remarks fell on deaf ears. She was sold to the highest bidder, the Hudson's Bay Company, for £10,000, about one-fourth of her original cost. Financial problems had forced the National Geographical Society to sell her to the famous Canadian trading company, who wanted *Discovery* because her reputation as an efficient ice-breaker (although the ship had spent months jammed in the ice of Antarctica and Scott himself had doubts about the efficacy of her work

FIG. 11.2
Scotia
SY *Scotia* trapped in the Weddell Sea
at 74 degrees 1 minute south.
Royal Scottish Geographical Society

in pack-ice). By the time of Scott's second expedition and his death in 1912, *Discovery* was operating as a cargo vessel operating from the UK West India Dock in London to Canada for the Company, via the Hudson Strait and James Bay, with furs forming the cargo on the return voyage.

Thereafter she had a number of different roles, including making use of her experience at high latitudes by carrying supplies to the White Russian forces during the Civil War. Following a major re-fit, *Discovery* resumed her career as a research vessel, operating for a spell out of the Falklands, researching whale stocks, and then in 1929 working once more in Antarctic waters. After 1931 she returned for good to home waters and occupied a number of roles, including as a training ship for the Sea Scouts and a drill ship for the Royal Naval Voluntary Reserve (post-war Royal Naval Reserve). Eventually the Maritime Trust assumed responsibility for the old ship on the Thames, until 1985, when the Dundee Heritage Trust took her over. She was welcomed back to the city that had built her, and *Discovery* now forms the focal point of the immensely popular Discovery Point visitor attraction.

The whaler *Terra Nova*, which had helped to break *Discovery* free in 1904, became Scott's own ship during his second and tragic expedition. Coincidentally, but not surprisingly, the tough little *Terra Nova* had also been built in Dundee.

EXPEDITIONS IN THE GREAT YEARS OF POLAR EXPLORATION

Expedition	Dates	Ship
Belgian Antarctic Expedition	1897–99	*Belgica*
British Antarctic Expedition	1898–1900	*Southern Cross*
German South Polar Expedition	1901–03	*Gauss*
Swedish South Polar Expedition	1901–04	*Antarctica*
British National Antarctic Expedition (Scott)	1901–04	*Discovery*
Scottish National Antarctic Expedition (Bruce)	1902–04	*Scotia*
French Antarctic Expedition	1903–04	*Francais*
British Antarctic Expedition (Shackleton)	1907–09	*Nimrod*
French Antarctic Expedition	1908–10	*Pourquoi-Pas*

Norwegian Antarctic Expedition (Amundsen*)	1910–12	*Fram*
British Antarctic Expedition (Scott d. 1912)	1910–13	*Terra Nova*
German South Polar Expedition	1911–12	*Deutschland*
Australian Antarctic Expedition	1911–14	*Aurora*
Imperial Trans-Antarctic Expedition (Shackleton)	1914–16	*Endurance*

* First to South Pole

Several references have been made in this chapter to the importance of the whalers built in Dundee in the development of the Scottish ship through history. Here is an extract from a book written a few years after the *Discovery*'s expedition to the Southern Ocean. It describes the whalers' enormous toil and many dangers in the most graphic of terms. The author was David Bone, a notable Glaswegian sea-captain and friend of the greatest of all maritime authors writing in English, Joseph Conrad:

> The whale ships, although they may not have seen one another since clearing the Tay, generally arrive together within a few days. Rumours of their presence on the coast get about. Fishermen report having seen them anchored, 'wind-bound' in some remote West Highland bay, or trawlers running in with their fish speak of having seen square sail to the nor'ard. Then glad hearts in Dundee read of their arrival; a bare, brief paragraph enough, but a wealth of incident to them. 'Lerwick, Nov., —, Dundee whaler *Diana* has put in; all well. She has three whales. Spoke Eclipse with a catch of four on Aug. 18.' A reassuring report to begin with, and one that augurs well for the rest of the fleet![2]

The whaling industry of Dundee, like that of Nantucket and other New England ports, gave birth to a rich harvest of folk songs like the 'Bonny Ship the *Diamond*', quoted in Chapter 1. Here is another shanty, in one of its several forms:

---

[2] Bone, David W, 'The Harvest of the North' from *Broken Stowage*, Duckworth, London, 1915

Dundee Whalers

Oh the noble fleet of whalers out sailing from Dundee,
Well manned by British sailors to work them on the sea;
On the western ocean passage none with them can compare
For there's not a ship could make the trip as the *Balena* I declare.

Refrain:

And the wind is on her quarter and her engine working free
  [OR the sails are full an' free]
And there's not another whaler a-sailing from Dundee
Can beat the aul' *Balena* and you needna try her on
For we challenge all both large and small from Dundee to St Johns.

There's the new built *Terra Nova*, she's a model with no doubt
There's the *Arctic* and *Aurora*, you've heard so much about
There's Jacklin's model mail-boat, the terror of the sea
Couldn't beat the aul *Balena* boys, on a passage from Dundee.

Refrain

And it happened on the Thursday four days after we left Dundee
Was carried off the quarter boats all in a raging sea
That took away our bulwark, our stanchions and our rails
And left the whole concern boys, a-floating in the gales.

Refrain

Bold Jacklin carries canvas and fairly raises steam
And Captain Guy's a daring boy, goes ploughing through the stream
But Millan says the *Eskimo* could beat the bloomin' lot
But to beat the aul' *Balena* boys, they'd find it rather hot.

Refrain

An' now that we've landed boys, where the rum is mighty cheap
We'll drink success to the Capt'n, for getting' us o'er the deep
And a health to all our sweathearts, an' to our wives so fair
Not another ship could make that trip but the *Balena* I declare.

Refrain

CHAPTER 12

Lusitania (1907–15)

THE ORIGINS OF THE great four-funnelled Cunard transatlantic liner *Lusitania* are more than usually complicated. This beautiful but expensive ship was built, like so many others for the same line, at John Brown's Clydebank yard. *Lusitania* was, however, different in that the need for a ship of this great size and speed was dictated by factors other than Cunard's commercial interests.

Ever since the start of regular transatlantic services there had been a natural and intense rivalry to have the fastest ship on the crossing. In the 60 years between the *Sirius*'s first steam crossing in 1838 to 1898, the Blue Riband, the title of fastest ship on the crossing, had been held, with just a gap from 1850–6, by British companies. Eleven Cunarders, six White Star ships, two each of the Guion Line and the Inman Line, and one each from the Great Western Steamship Company and the British and American Steam Navigation Company had held the record for westbound crossings. The 1850–6 gap was filled by two steamers of the US Collins Line. British supremacy on the Atlantic was seen as just another part of Britain's mercantile and imperial dominance – Britannia indeed ruled the waves.

It came as a blow to national pride and as a troubling indicator, for the perceptive, of the rising industrial, political and military power of Germany when, in 1898, the Blue Riband was taken from Cunard's *Lucania* by Norddeutscher Lloyd's *Kaiser Wilhelm der Grosse*. Norddeutscher held the prize for two years only to lose it to the Hamburg Amerika Line's *Deutschland*, but recaptured it in 1902 with the *Kronprinz Wilhelm*. From 1903 to 1907 the *Deutschland* again held the Blue Riband. The *Lucania*'s best speed for the westbound crossing was 21.81 knots, the 1903 speed for the *Deutschland* was 23.15 knots.

Speed was a matter for commercial pride, and Cunard would in 1910 advertise that they had 'the largest and fastest vessels in the world' but speed was only one component in passenger choice. Reliability, comfort, catering, style and image were just as important. The time saved by the extra 1.34 knots that the *Deutschland* could steam at was actually not all that significant.

However, speed had a significant strategic importance. In event of a war if the *Deutschland* or *Kronprinz Wilhelm* were to become commerce raiders, would the Royal Navy have ships that could catch them? There certainly were extremely fast warships in the Royal Navy of 1907 – but these were small ships, destroyers. Typical were the Tribal class destroyers built between 1905 and 1908; 1000-ton ships with limited endurance and whose top speed of 33 knots was seriously limited by adverse weather. The large warships of the day, capable of cruising the oceans in all weathers, were actually slower than the fastest Atlantic liners. The following table reveals the situation.

Lusitania and Contemporary Royal Navy Ships

Ship	Date	Length OA	Beam	GRT	IHP	Engine	Speed (knots)
RMS *Lusitania*	1907	762.2	87.8	31,550	67,000	Turbine	26
HMS *Commonwealth* Edward VII Class Battleship	1905	567	78.9	20,135	18,000	Triple Exp.	19
HMS *Dreadnought* Dreadnought Class Battleship	1906	527	82	20,730	24,712	Turbine	21
HMS *Duke of Edinburgh* Armoured Cruiser	1906	505.5	73.5	13,550	23,000	Triple Exp.	23
HMS *Temeraire* Bellerophon Class Battleship	1909	526	82.5	22,540	23,000	Turbine	21
RMS *Aquitania*	1913	868.7	97	45,646	56,000	Turbine	24

In the 1880s the Admiralty had entered into arrangements with Cunard and the rival White Star Line for the payment of a subsidy on some of their fastest liners. The subsidy at the rate of 15 shillings per gross register ton a year ensured that the Admiralty could take up these ships as armed merchant cruisers in the event of a crisis. The ships chosen had to be capable of mounting 4.7-inch guns, have internal sub-division of their hull space to Admiralty standards and have steering-gear below the waterline. The latter two provisos were to ensure survivability from shell damage. The companies had to build gun platforms on their decks and ensure that 50 per cent of the crew were Royal Navy reservists and to have the ships available for conversion within a week. This obviously meant that ships which were engaged on long-distance routes to Australia or India were unsuitable but fast ships on the North Atlantic with a shorter voyage time were ideal candidates. The scheme offered a valuable subsidy to these British companies, faced with increasingly tough competition, and made available a group of fast auxiliary cruisers to the Admiralty at a fraction of the cost of building such vessels.

In addition to the potential use of these ships as armed merchant cruisers they were potentially valuable as troopships. The advantage of an 18-knot Atlantic liner over a 12-knot troopship on a long passage carrying urgently needed reinforcements to some imperial trouble spot was significant.

Such was the relationship between speed and engine power that these fast liners, if operated on patrol duties at economical speed as armed merchant cruisers, would have extremely long endurance and could stay at sea for many weeks without refuelling.

One of the factors in the speed competition on the North Atlantic was that every additional knot of speed achieved was only gained at an enormous increase in size of ship and engine power. In 1902 an Admiralty Committee on mercantile cruisers produced a most revealing table showing the alarming costs of moving from a 20-knot liner to a 26-knot liner:

Average Ocean Speed in Knots	First cost of building	Engine Power IHP	Annual Subsidy Required
20	£350,000	19,000	£9,000
21	£400,000	22,000	£19,500
22	£470,000	25,500	£40,500
23	£575,000	30,000	£67,500
24	£850,000	40,000	£110,500
25	£1,000,000	52,000	£149,000
26	£1,250,000	68,000	£204,000

The Blue Riband was held, when this report was issued in December 1902, by the *Kronprinz Wilhelm* with a Westbound speed of 23.09 knots – to seize this record from the Germans would involve the investment of a huge sum of money, money which could not be justified on commercial grounds by Cunard.

The situation became even more complicated in 1902–03 with the formation, by the American tycoon J. Pierpont Morgan, of the International Mercantile Marine Company. This US-owned conglomerate brought together various US and British shipping lines, including the owners of the White Star Line. The Morgan syndicate would later create alliances with the Norddeutscher Lloyd and Hamburg-Amerika lines. This move not only threatened Cunard's place on the North Atlantic but concerns were expressed in Parliament, and elsewhere, that the takeover could remove the Admiralty-subsidised White Star ships from British control. In fact, the White Star and other British ships owned by the Morgan combine continued to sail under the Red Ensign and a new agreement was signed in August 1903 continuing the Admiralty's pre-emptive rights on these vessels. There was still some unease about the situation and about the German competition and discussions took place between the Admiralty and Cunard's Chairman, Lord Inverclyde, about building new large and fast ships for the Atlantic crossing to outclass the German ships.

The speed required, as the table above indicated, made these ships commercially impossible for Cunard and the existing subsidy arrangement would not address the issues of the hugely inflated capital and running costs. After lengthy negotiations involving Cunard, the Admiralty, the Board of Trade, the Post Office (who were concerned with the Mails contract) and the Treasury, Lord Inverclyde was able to announce to his shareholders at an Extraordinary General Meeting held at Liverpool on 29 July 1903 that a deal had been struck.

The essential points of this agreement were that Cunard would build two new very large steamships of high speed for the Atlantic trade, that they and the rest of the Cunard fleet were at the government's disposal for charter or purchase on equitable terms. For its part, the government would provide a loan at favourable rates (2.75% against the prevailing commercial rate of 5%) of £2.4 million repayable over 20 years – in effect, a huge subsidy to Cunard to compensate for the inflated capital costs of building a 26-knot liner. The higher running costs would be compensated for by an annual payment of £150,000. Cunard's articles of association would require to be altered to ensure that it continued to be a British concern with regard to ships, ownership, management and control.

The deal went through Parliament in August 1903 at the end of the Commons session, despite grumblings about the favoured treatment Cunard were receiving. However, the weight of opinion was that the deal was a good one for the government. Indeed, as all 19 fast steamers in the Cunard fleet were subject to government requisition the annual subsidy was a modest one when spread over all the vessels. As Hugh Arnold-Foster, the Financial Secretary to the Admiralty, pointed out, what was being paid for the two vessels was less than half the cost of a third-class cruiser. Arnold-Foster also summed up the need for the ships: 'What would be the position if in a naval war no vessel carrying the British flag could cope with cruisers such as those we might find employed against us?'

The plans for the new ship evolved with the Cunard design department working with four potential builders. The design was refined through extensive experimental tank testing that showed that a broader hull and more power would be needed to meet the required speed level. The dimensions of the new ships increased as a result of this work and two of the yards, Vickers at Barrow and Fairfield at Govan could no longer undertake to build such a ship. The contracts for the two new ships, which followed the Cunard tradition of having geographical names ending in IA, *Mauretania* and *Lusitania* (Roman provinces in North Africa and Portugal), went to two of Cunard's regular shipbuilders. *Mauretania* would be built on Tyneside at Swan Hunter & Whigham Richardson while *Lusitania* would become the 33rd Cunarder to be built by John Brown & Co., Clydebank, or its predecessor J. & G. Thomson.

Quite how much of a leap forward was being taken is revealed by a comparison between *Lusitania* and some earlier Cunarders on the North Atlantic service.

Ship	Date	Length	Beam	Tonnage	Horsepower
Britannia	1841	207	34.2	1,154	740
Etruria	1884	501.5	57.2	8,120	14,500
Lucania	1893	601	65.2	12,950	30,000
Saxonia	1900	580	64.2	14,280	10,000
Carmania	1905	650.4	72.2	19,524	21,000
Lusitania	1907	762.2	87.8	31,550	67,000

This giant ship was designed to accommodate around 550 first class, 500 second class and over 1,200 third class passengers and would have a crew of over 800 – all told, over 3,000 people would be on board when she was fully laden.

After considerable deliberation, and the advice of an expert committee, it was decided to employ turbine machinery in the new ship. This was a new form of propulsion, invented by Charles Parsons, and demonstrated in his *Turbinia* of 1897. The expert panel that Cunard assembled included Parsons, Rear-Admiral Oram, the Deputy Engineer in Chief of the Navy, and Walter Brock, the senior partner in the Dumbarton shipbuilders William Denny & Bros, the builders of the first commercial turbine ship, the 1901 Clyde steamer *King Edward*. See photo 16.3.

Turbine propulsion works by directing high-pressure steam on to a series of blades operating within a casing – the turbine blades are then linked by reduction gearing to the ship's propellers. *Lusitania* would have four turbines each driving one shaft and propeller – additionally two turbines were connected to the central shafts for going astern. Twenty-five boilers fed by 192 coal-fired furnaces provided the steam for this array of turbines. *Lusitania* was not Cunard's first venture into turbine propulsion – the *Carmania* had been built at Clydebank and launched in 1905.

Lusitania was launched on 7 June 1907 by Mary, Lady Inverclyde, widow of the Second Lord Inverclyde, who had died a few months earlier. Because of the great size of the ship special measures had to be taken to widen the river opposite the yard. At the post-launch luncheon Sir Charles McLaren, deputy-chairman of John Brown & Co., observed that the ship they had just seen launched:

> In length, breadth, depth and capacity… exceeded any other vessel that had ever been designed, whilst her engine power would be such as to send her across the Atlantic at a speed never yet accomplished, except by a torpedo-boat destroyer… It might be made with very slight alterations the fastest and most powerful cruiser in the world. The Government were well justified in standing at the back of an enterprise of this kind.

He went on to underline the significance of the international rivalry on the North Atlantic:

He felt that no one present would be satisfied that for capacity and speed of the Atlantic liners the record should be held by Germany. Britain was the mistress of the seas; we had always been in the lead in marine construction, and there was not a Briton who ought not to feel proud that this launch had once more placed Great Britain in the forefront of marine architecture.

In July 1907 *Lusitania* left the Clyde on a trial cruise round Ireland to her home port of Liverpool. On subsequent trials she proved to be capable of a sustained speed of over 26 knots and an average speed over 1,200 miles of 25.4 knots, so the contractual obligation to sustain an Atlantic speed of 24.5 knots was likely to be easily achieved, if not exceeded.

However, one problem emerged on the trials – at high speed the stern compartments, occupied by second class passengers, were subject to excessive vibration caused by the high-speed propellers, which were a feature of the turbine drive. A refit of this area and extensive stiffening had to be undertaken.

The 'floating palace', with interior design by the Glasgow architect James Millar who found his inspiration in Georgian and Louis XVI styles, sailed on her maiden transatlantic voyage from Liverpool to New York on 7 September 1907.

The Times correspondent on board filed copy from the first port of call, Queenstown (now Cobh) in County Cork, Ireland, where the liner lay off the harbour and passengers and mail were loaded. Of the scenes at Liverpool, with crowds which a colleague estimated at 200,000, he wrote:

> It was an inspiriting scene, and the Cunard Line must realise more than ever before how much their enterprise is appreciated, and how strongly both Liverpool and British sentiment is supporting their endeavours to recover for British ships the Atlantic fastest record now held by Germany.

From Ireland the *Lusitania* then sailed direct to the Sandy Hook Light off New York. On this maiden voyage her speed reached an average of 23.01 knots, a little below the *Deutschland*'s record of 23.58 knots – this comparatively modest speed was attributable to the combination of fog and a natural desire not to push the new machinery too hard on its first crossing. On a subsequent crossing *Lusitania* edged past the German ship's record and recorded a speed of 23.61 knots and held, albeit briefly, the Blue Riband.

She was to lose the eastbound record later in 1907 when her sister ship, the *Mauretania*, came into service. Despite being designed to identical standards by Cunard's staff, a degree of flexibility had been granted to the builders and the *Mauretania* was always to be the slightly faster ship and her record speed of 26.25 eastbound secured the Blue Riband for Britain and Cunard until 1929. The *Lusitania* retained the westbound record with a speed of 25.65 knots until 1909 when the *Mauretania* moved ahead with a speed of 26.06 knots. Despite this speed difference, the *Lusitania* was the more popular of the two great sisters – her lighter interior décor pleased passengers more than the rather dark oak and mahogany favoured by the *Mauretania*'s interior designer.

The seven years of peace saw *Lusitania* continue as a very popular part of the Atlantic service, with an interruption in 1913 caused by damaged turbine blades.

On the outbreak of war in August 1914, after an initial cessation of services, normal transatlantic services soon resumed. Despite all the plans to use the *Lusitania* as an armed merchant cruiser, she was not in fact called up for service and continued to operate her traditional Liverpool to New York route in company with other ships transferred from the Boston route such as the *Franconia*. Her much larger Clydebank-built stablemate *Aquitania* was swiftly converted to be a merchant cruiser and then just as swiftly re-employed as a troop transport and a number of the slightly smaller Cunarders like the *Carmania* did find employment as auxiliary cruisers.

The reduction in traffic caused by the war resulted in a consolidation of services and by December 1914 Cunard were advertising the sailing of *Lusitania* on a monthly service to New York with the other sailings being operated by ships like the Anchor Line's *Cameronia* and *Transylvania* – Cunard had taken over the Anchor Line in 1911. Top speed was hardly justified with low passenger numbers and so Cunard took the decision to sail at lower speed. This enabled savings in coal and labour when a quarter of the boilers were shut down and maximum speed was reduced to 21 knots.

On Saturday 30 January 1915 *Lusitania* sailed from New York for Liverpool, arriving in the Mersey on Saturday 6 February wearing not

Cunard Liner "LUSITANIA" (Turbine).

32,000 Tons ; 68,000 H.P. ; Speed 26¼ knots

Length 787 ft. ; Breadth 88 ft. ; Depth 60 ft.

FIG. 12.1
Lusitania from a pre First World War postcard.
Authors Collection

the Red Ensign, but the American flag. Admiralty instructions had been received when she was off the Irish coast that, because of the risk of attack by German submarines, she should complete her journey under American colours. It was pointed out that there was no illegality in this procedure as *Lusitania* was carrying American passengers and mails – but the incident raised questions, particularly among the more isolationist elements in the United States.

At this time the German government, arguing that Britain had too widely interpreted pre-war agreements on contraband and neutral shipping in time of war, and as Britain was attempting to starve Germany by imposing blockade, now declared:

> ... all the waters surrounding Great Britain and Ireland, including the English Channel, as an area of war, thus proceeding against the shipping of the enemy.

And warned that:

> ... from February 18 1915, it will endeavour to destroy every enemy merchant ship that is found in this area of war without it always being possible to avert the peril that this threatens persons and cargoes. Neutrals are therefore warned against further entrusting crews and passengers and wares to such ships.

The statement went on to advise neutral flag ships to avoid this area as, although German ships were instructed to avoid damage to neutrals, the British abuse of neutral flags and the exigencies of warfare made it impossible to guarantee their safety when attacks were being made against enemy shipping. A safe zone was declared North of Shetland and in the Eastern part of the North Sea.

This was a significant departure from the norms of international law – the threat to sink British and allied merchant ships without warning in the waters around the British Isles was on the face of it a serious one. At this stage in the war merchant shipping was still sailing unescorted, the introduction of convoys had to wait for a later period when German submarines had become a very real threat to national survival. British shipowners initially took the German warning as an empty threat – assuming that no civilised state would descend to sinking merchant ships without warning.

On 1 May, the German Embassy in Washington published an advertisement in US newspapers:

> Travellers intending to embark for an Atlantic voyage are reminded that a state of war exists between Germany and her Allies and Great Britain and her Allies; that the zone of war includes the waters adjacent to the British Isles; that in accordance with the formal notice given by the Imperial German Government vessels flying the flag of Great Britain or any of her Allies are liable to destruction in those waters; and that travellers sailing in the war zone in ships of Great Britain and her Allies do so at their own risk.

On the same day *Lusitania* sailed from New York on what should have been her 202nd Atlantic crossing – included in her complement were three Germans who were found on board with a camera and who were suspected of being spies. The three luckless Germans were confined in the ship's cells and went down with the ship. The total of passengers, crew and prisoners amounted to 1962 – considerably below her maximum capacity, even allowing for the reduction in third class accommodation made at the outbreak of war to allow for more cargo space. She was also carrying 1,200 tons of general cargo, including 173 tons of rifle ammunition and 4,992 3-inch artillery shells. *Lusitania*, on this round trip, was under the command of Captain William R. Turner, normally the master of the *Aquitania*, currently serving as an armed merchant cruiser, but now acting as a relief for the *Lusitania's* usual skipper, Captain Daniel Dow.

The United States was very concerned to maintain its neutrality and there were normally prohibitions on the carrying of explosives in passenger ships but the US Department of Commerce had given permission for the transport of this ammunition. A close inspection was made of the ships of belligerents in US ports and the later German claim that *Lusitania* had concealed guns mounted and that Canadian troops were being carried – either of which, if true, could have made her a legitimate target, was strenuously denied by the United States. A senior US government official at New York Port later declared that *Lusitania* had no guns of any calibre or description on any deck and that if any individual reservists sailed on her they did so as individuals paying their own passage.

The *Lusitania's* passage was uneventful, although influenced by war conditions, and the German Embassy's note did not seem to have unduly alarmed the passengers. Making her way at the war economy speed of 21 knots, watertight doors shut, and a proportion of the ship's boats swung out ready for emergencies, with extra look-outs posted, Captain Turner considered that he had taken all appropriate precautions. As the ship approached the Old Head of Kinsale in Ireland on 7 May 1915 her speed had been reduced to 18 knots – probably to ensure that she arrived in the Mersey just in time to catch the tide. The easiest target for a submarine was a stationary ship at a predictable location, such as the mouth of the Mersey.

Even at 18 knots *Lusitania* could have outrun a pursuing submarine, but 14 miles off land the German submarine U-20 commanded by Kapitänleutnant Walther Schwieger was in position and, without warning, fired one or more torpedoes at the Cunard liner.

The British official enquiry into the sinking found that two torpedoes struck *Lusitania* on her starboard side and a third torpedo aimed at the port side missed. Persistent reports, however, suggest that only one torpedo struck the ship and the second explosion was caused by the detonation of her explosive cargo. Two explosions were certainly noted, and a seaman, giving evidence to the enquiry, clearly testified that he had sighted two torpedo tracks. Lord Mersey, the Wreck Commissioner, after hearing evidence from all possible witness and having the benefit of a team of naval assessors and a large range of counsel for all the interested parties concluded there was no explosion of the cargo and that the sinking was due solely to the torpedoes. However, German sources suggest that U-20 only fired one torpedo and that the second and fatal explosion was caused by either ammunition exploding or coal dust exploding. The matter, though interesting, is in the long run irrelevant – whatever caused the second explosion was either a second torpedo or the effects of the first torpedo.

Many passengers on board were American citizens and 128 of them lost their lives. The eventual death toll was 1,201 lives – a loss which was perhaps higher than might have been expected and was partly caused by the explosions shattering the main steam pipes making it impossible to reverse engines. The ship was thus forced to sail on for 10 minutes, making lowering of boats more difficult. The list she took on also meant that the starboard lifeboats were unusable.

The sinking caused outrage in Britain and in the United States but was greeted in Germany as a bold stroke of war. The *Frankfurter Zeitung* was reported by *The Times* to have observed:

FIG. 12.2
An artist's impression by Charles Nixon of the sinking of the Lusitania.
Authors' Collection

A German warship has destroyed the *Lusitania* off the coast of Ireland. An enormous property, which weighed against us in the enemy's scale, has been annihilated. Many millions of material property have been destroyed, and immeasurable possessions in moral strength and sentiment of a people whose whole life is staked upon the prosperity of its shipping and its trade sank with the proud vessel.

The *Lusitania* was not the first merchant vessel to have been sunk by German submarines. The Elder Dempster liner *Falaba* was stopped on 28 March and her crew and passengers given five minutes to abandon ship – however, a high sea was running and many of the ship's boats swamped or were smashed in lowering and around 110 lives were lost. The US oil tanker *Gulflight* was sunk without warning, with the loss of three lives, west of the Scillies on 1 May bound for Rouen, France. However, the fame of the *Lusitania,* the scale of the tragedy, the lack of warning, and the death of so many prominent American citizens made this a particularly potent incident.

If the German submarine commander had identified the *Lusitania* as an armed auxiliary flying the White Ensign and in effect a Royal Navy ship, then he had a legitimate target. If he believed her to be a merchant vessel carrying contraband in the shape of ammunition then he was entitled under international conventions to seize her. The most recent convention covering this topic, the Treaty of London 1909, had never grappled with the problem of how a submarine was supposed to take as a prize a 32,000-ton ocean liner. The enforcement of a blockade by submarines more or less necessitated the sinking of the enemy vessel, with, it was assumed, proper provision made for the safe evacuation of her crew and passengers. This could only be done by the submarine surfacing and hailing the vessel – of course, if Kapitänleutnant Schwieger thought that *Lusitania* was armed with a dozen 4.7-inch guns he would have been understandably reluctant to expose his frail submarine to her gunfire.

The schedule of Cunard ships was a matter of public knowledge, of public advertisement in fact, even in wartime, and Schwieger, if he identified the ship correctly, should have known that the United States would not have received her as a civilian ship had she been converted to a merchant cruiser, and he cannot have been aware of the contents of *Lusitania*'s hold. The presence of artillery shells and rifle ammunition may be a *post facto* justification of his action but it could not have been known at the time he launched the torpedo.

US President Wilson sent a strongly worded note to the German government condemning the attack on the *Lusitania*, insisting on the impossibility of using submarines to enforce an economic blockade in a manner compatible with the accepted rules of justice and humanity, seeking reparation for the loss of US lives and property, and threatening that his government would take 'any act necessary to the performance of its sacred duty of maintaining the rights of the United States and its citizens'. The note also offered an escape clause for the German government by suggesting that the sinking was carried out by an officer who had misunderstood the orders of the high command and suggesting that the German government should disavow the officer and his actions.

The German government responded to the US note, regretting the loss of US lives, but adding:

> ... the *Lusitania* was one of the largest and fastest British merchant ships built with Government funds as an auxiliary cruiser and was carried expressly as such in the Navy List issued by the British Admiralty.

This was, of course, perfectly true, but the *Lusitania*'s role as a civilian passenger transport was known to anyone, including the German government, with access to the daily press. The German note went on to claim, after pointing out that many British merchant ships had guns fitted and naval gunners on board:

> The *Lusitania*, too, according to information received here, had cannon on board which were mounted and concealed under the deck.

This was untrue. *Lusitania* had been fitted in 1913 with gun mountings, but not with guns, and her sailings from New York would have been impossible had she had guns mounted openly or covertly, the US authorities would have considered her a warship and she would have been interned.

Wilson was passionately committed to US neutrality, and in a speech a few days after the *Lusitania* sinking spoke of 'being too proud to fight'. The sinking of the *Lusitania* is often cited as the reason why the United States entered the war – this is undoubtedly much too simplistic a connection. *Lusitania* was torpedoed in May 1915, Wilson won the presidential election in November 1916 on a non-interventionist platform, and American only declared war on Germany after many further provocations, including the introduction of unrestricted U-boat warfare, in April 1917. However, the sinking of the *Lusitania* undoubtedly played a significant role in swinging American opinion, which had been largely hostile to the British blockade of Germany, against the German cause.

CHAPTER 13

HMS *Hood* (1918–41)

QUITE WHY SOME SHIPS become iconic is unclear. Size, function, grace of line, fitness for purpose all must surely have some part in the process, but there does need to be an additional feature that makes one particular ship stand out from the generality.

For all of her life the battle cruiser HMS *Hood* was undoubtedly an icon – 'the mighty *Hood*' represented the Royal Navy and the nation as no other ship of her day did. Whether this status would have been attained had her three sister ships of the planned Admiral class of battle cruisers – *Howe*, *Rodney* and *Anson* – ever emerged from the three yards that were commissioned in April and July 1916 to build them is debatable. In the event work on the other three ships was suspended in March 1917 and they were cancelled in October 1918.

The origins of the class go back to October 1915 when the Admiralty ordered designs to be produced for a new class of battleship featuring reduced draught and the latest anti-torpedo protection. Over the succeeding few months the design brief evolved into a class of large battle cruisers offering high speed and heavy armament, but with less protective armour than a battleship.

The modern battleship's origins are usually seen in Fisher's *Dreadnought* of 1907. Admiral Sir John Arbuthnot 'Jacky' Fisher, First Sea Lord from 1904–10, did much to modernise the Royal Navy and the introduction of the *Dreadnought* class of battleships was one major step in this process. The essential feature of the *Dreadnought* was a concentration on a main armament of big guns – 10 12-inch guns mounted in five twin turrets with just light secondary armament to deter torpedo boats. Earlier battleships had mounted a variety of guns of different calibre – for example, the *Majestic* class of 1894–7 had been equipped with four 12-inch guns in two twin turrets, 12 6-inch guns, and smaller weapons. *Dreadnought* and later battleships were fitted with the new steam turbine engine developed by Charles Parsons and demonstrated in *Turbinia* in 1897. The turbine engine gave greater power for less weight of machinery and permitted *Dreadnought* to make 21½ knots as against the 16 knots of the *Majestics*. However Fisher's real hope was pinned on an even faster vessel combining the striking power of the most modern battleship but with significantly higher speed. Something had to be sacrificed in this design and armour protection was reduced. This new class of ship became known as the battle cruiser and to Fisher and his supporters it represented the modern embodiment of the Nelsonian spirit of dash and daring. Fisher believed that the battle cruiser, armed with heavy guns and having a marked speed advantage, could hit enemy battleships hard and at long range, and thus obviate the problem of their weaker armour. The theory was good, the practical problems of fire control and target spotting at long range were, however, considerable.

Fisher's first class of battle cruisers – the three *Invincible* class ships ordered in 1906 mounted eight 12-inch guns and could reach 26 knots but had thinner armour than the 21-knot British battleships ordered at the same time.

Technology moved on swiftly and by 1915 it was possible to consider the construction of a 33-knot battle cruiser, and from this design concept came HMS *Hood*.

Hood's design evolved in the light of experience gained at the Battle of Jutland, 31 May 1916, where the Royal Navy lost three battle cruisers from a battle cruiser force of nine ships – Jutland was an expensive victory, with profound questions being raised about the design and performance of the British capital ships. As Admiral David Beatty, commander of the battle cruiser force, said to his flag captain A. E. Chatfield when he saw the battle cruisers *Indefatigable* and *Queen Mary* explode and sink with great loss of life: 'There's something wrong with our bloody ships today'. Improvements were made to the deck, magazine and turret protection by the Admiralty team under the Director of Naval Construction, Sir Eustace Tennyson d'Eyncourt, and in response to comments from Admiral Jellicoe, commanding the Grand Fleet, and Admiral Beatty.

Hood's significance is suggested by a few statistics. The last class of battleships laid down before *Hood* – the *Royal Sovereigns* – were 620 feet long and had a displacement of 29,150 tons and cost around £2.5 million. Two planned battleships were redesigned as battle cruisers following the Battle of the Falklands in December 1914. These ships, *Repulse* and *Renown*, were significantly bigger than the *Royal Sovereigns* at 794 feet and 30,700 tons, and cost £3.1 million and could steam at 31.5 knots. (These figures are for *Renown,* which was built at Fairfield's yard on the Clyde – *Repulse* being a product of John Brown's yard.) *Hood,* armed with eight 15-inch guns, 860 feet long and 42,100 tons would be the largest capital ship in the world and cost a staggering £6 million.

The *Glasgow Herald* in January 1920 observed that *Hood* was designated a battle cruiser but commented:

> ... it is doubtful whether the term battleship is not equally accurate. The vessel is so much a departure from all previous practice in the construction of capital ships, and she stands so much alone in the navies of the world that she would call for a designation devoted to herself exclusively.

However, the fact remained that *Hood* did not have the level of armour protection that was enjoyed by battleships. The post-Jutland analysis of Royal Navy losses and the significantly greater survivability of German capital ships resulted in further increases in armour protection being provided for *Hood* while she was still in course of construction.

After trials in Spring 1920 *Hood* was finally accepted from the builders on 15 May and sailed for Plymouth, where on 18 May she became the Flagship of the Battle Cruiser Squadron of the Atlantic Fleet, flying the flag of Rear Admiral Sir Roger Keyes.

Hood settled into the routine of the post-war Navy with showing-the-flag tours, and the general run of exercises, training, fleet regattas, as well as a variety of one-off tasks, such as providing a Marine guard of honour for the burial of the Unknown Warrior at Westminster Abbey on 11 November 1920 or finding a force to render assistance to the civil powers in Cowdenbeath and Dunfermline during transport and coal strikes in April 1921.

Hood starred in one of the Royal Navy's most successful 'flag-showing' ventures – the round-the-world cruise of the Special Service Squadron in 1923/24. *Hood,* in company with her Clydebank-built consort *Repulse* and the 1st Light Cruiser Squadron, carried out what was the Royal Navy's first planned circumnavigation since the age of sail. Sailing from Devonport on 27 November, the Squadron, under Vice Admiral Sir Frederick L. Field, called at colonies and dominions in West, South and East Africa before heading to Ceylon, Malaya and Singapore. Visits to

FIG. 13.1

HMS *Hood* leaving the fitting out basin at John Brown's.

Glasgow University Archives

ports in Australia and New Zealand were carried out before cruising to Fiji, Hawaii, British Columbia and down to San Francisco. The Squadron then split with the light cruisers visiting South America and rounding Cape Horn, while the two battle cruisers transited the Panama Canal (*Hood*'s canal dues came to $22,399.50) and then sailed to Canada with a stop on the way at Jamaica. After successful visits to Halifax, Quebec and Newfoundland the battle cruisers sailed for Devonport, rendezvousing with the cruiser squadron off the *Lizard*. The combined squadron arrived back at Devonport on 29 September having steamed 38,152 miles. During the course of this mission over three quarters of a million visitors came on board the *Hood* – adding greatly to her status as 'the mighty *Hood*' and in a very real sense the embodiment of the interwar Royal Navy.

After this cruise there was doubtless much work to be done in her annual refit – a ship of this size and complexity required significant annual maintenance. *Hood* would spend the remainder of the 1920s and the 1930s in a round of exercises, cruises, manoeuvres and routine refits. In May 1929 she paid off and went into Portsmouth Royal Naval Dockyard for a major refit and did not take her place again in the active fleet until May 1931, when she commissioned with a Portsmouth crew (having previously been a Devonport manned ship) as flagship of the Battle Cruiser Squadron of the Atlantic Fleet. In the long-term plans of the Admiralty this refit gave *Hood* another 10 years' life expectancy as a modern and effective unit of the battle fleet – her eventual replacement would become due in 1941. Among the changes made at this time was the provision of two pom-poms, eight-barrelled two-pounder anti-aircraft guns. These guns, with their high rate of fire, reflected the growing concern about air-attack – a threat which had, of course, barely existed when *Hood* was designed and her anti-aircraft armament would be progressively increased in future years.

In 1931 *Hood* was involved in the Invergordon Mutiny, and Rear Admiral Wilfrid Tomkinson, commanding the Battle Cruiser Squadron of the Atlantic Fleet, found himself in the middle of a very unpleasant situation. The Flag Officer commanding the Atlantic Fleet had been hospitalised and Tomkinson, flying his flag in *Hood,* was in temporary command of the fleet, which was in September of 1931 concentrated at Invergordon. A national financial crisis had caused the government to propose an overall reduction in the pay of the armed forces. News of this leaked out in a garbled form but the essential message of a 10 per cent cut was true. Sailors on board most of the ships of the Atlantic Fleet, including *Hood,* refused to leave harbour on scheduled training. The issue of the pay cut was undoubtedly badly handled by the Admiralty with incomplete information being distributed erratically. Eventually the proposed pay cut was withdrawn, a number of the mutineers were dismissed the service, and Tomkinson became the scapegoat for the mutiny with the Admiralty believing that he could have taken more vigorous steps to quell the mutiny. His career ended with his being retired as a Vice Admiral in 1932.

In 1935 *Hood* was urgently despatched to Gibraltar as part of the Royal Navy's build-up in the Mediterranean in response to the Italian invasion of Abyssinia and plans to enforce the League of Nations sanctions against Italy.

From 1936 to 1939 *Hood* was to spend much of her time in the

Mediterranean and off the Spanish coast on duties connected with the world powers' attempt to confine the Spanish Civil War to that country.

In 1939 *Hood* underwent a substantial refit at Portsmouth Royal Naval Dockyard from January to August and at the end of August was, with the rest of the Royal Navy, mobilised for war. *Hood* and the Battle Cruiser Squadron (*Renown* and *Repulse*) sailed for Scapa Flow and thence to patrol the Iceland/Faeroes passage. Two days after the outbreak of war she narrowly avoided a German torpedo and on 26 September was hit by a 500 pound bomb dropped from a Junkers 88 bomber and sustained slight damage. Much of the rest of 1939 was occupied in patrols in the North Sea. The fleet base at Scapa Flow was demonstrated to be unsafe when Gunther Prien took U-47 into the anchorage and torpedoed *Royal Oak* on 14 October, with the loss of 833 lives. As a result, *Hood* and the rest of the Home Fleet was redeployed to Loch Ewe and the Clyde until the defences of Scapa Flow could be improved.

December 1939 found *Hood* at Greenock – on 13 December she was ordered out in company with *Warspite, Barham* and a destroyer escort following intelligence of a strong German force in the North Sea. There was concern that this German force was intended to enter the Atlantic and intercept the first Canadian troop convoy of the war. This convoy, carrying over 7,000 men of the 1st Canadian Division, comprised five large ex-passenger liners including the *Aquitania,* and had been allocated a Home Fleet destroyer escort. This would have been inadequate to deal with the three German cruisers and their accompanying destroyers so the *Hood* and her consorts were despatched to escort the convoy into the Clyde.

The early months of 1940 found *Hood* based on the Clyde and carrying out patrols in the Shetland/Faeroes passage. In February the German submarine U-33 penetrated the Clyde on a mine-laying mission. A survivor of the U-33 has suggested that the primary target for this highly risky mission was HMS *Hood*. The submarine was detected and sunk off Arran and the only German attempt to enter the target-rich environment of the Clyde resulted in the death of 25 of her crew.

After some necessary repairs, including re-tubing of her boilers, carried out at Devonport and Liverpool in April to June 1940, *Hood* sailed on 12 June to cover a major Australian and New Zealand troop convoy consisting of the liners *Queen Mary, Empress of Britain, Aquitania, Mauretania, Empress of Canada* and *Andes.*

Italy entered the war on 10 June 1940 and added a further challenge to the seriously overstretched Royal Navy. Later in June *Hood* left the Home Fleet and sailed for Gibraltar. On 28 June Force H was constituted at Gibraltar under Vice Admiral Sir James Somerville with the mission of containing the Italian Fleet within the Mediterranean and to carry out actions against the Italians. Later the task of covering the passage of Mediterranean convoys, in cooperation with the Commander in Chief Mediterranean Fleet, Admiral Sir A. B. Cunningham, based at Alexandria, was added to its remit, as were occasional operations in the North Atlantic. Force H was initially centred on the carrier *Ark Royal,* with the battleships *Resolution* and *Valiant,* and supporting cruisers and destroyers. Its constituent elements varied from time to time. On 30 June Admiral Somerville hoisted his flag in *Hood* and set about the distasteful but necessary task of neutralising the French fleet at the port of Mers-el-Kebir, near Oran, Algeria.

With the fall of France and the signing of an armistice on 25 June the danger was that the Vichy French government under Marshal Petain might allow the powerful French Mediterranean Fleet – which was split between Algeria and Alexandria – to cooperate with Germany or allow it to be taken over by Germany. There was a real threat to the Royal Navy's control of the Mediterranean, and indeed to the wider struggle, had, for example the modern battle cruisers *Dunkerque* and *Strasbourg* at Oran, fallen into German hands. There were, in addition, two older battleships, and numerous other ships in Mers-el-Kebir, Oran and Algiers.

Until the fall of France the Royal Navy and the French Navy had fought side by side – now Admiral Gensoul, commanding the French fleet in Algeria, was to be presented with four choices – to join Britain in the struggle against the Axis powers, to sail with his ships to a British port where the French ships would be interned for the duration of the war, to sail to a French West Indian colony and have the ships demilitarised there, or to have them sunk by the Royal Navy. A fifth option, less satisfactory from the British point of view, was to be accepted if he proposed it and rejected all other options – demilitarisation in Oran on condition that this could be satisfactorily done and a long-term neutralisation of the battle cruisers could be achieved.

Hood and Force H lay off the Algerian coast while an officer carried the British ultimatum to Gensoul. Churchill had signalled to Somerville 'You are charged with one of the most disagreeable and difficult tasks a British Admiral has ever been faced with...' and so it proved. At the other end of the Mediterranean, Gensoul's colleague, Admiral Godfroy, would agree to the demilitarisation of his ships, but Gensoul would only offer a promise that the ships would not fall intact into German or Italian hands but would not agree to their immediate demilitarisation – he also made preparations to take his squadron to sea, thus forcing the hand of the British commander, under pressure from London to achieve a swift resolution of the affair. Just before 6pm on 3 July, *Hood*, *Valiant* and *Resolution* opened fire with their 15-inch guns on their former allies.

In 10 minutes firing the battleship *Bretagne* had been sunk, the *Dunkerque* and the battleship *Provence* run aground. The French ships and shore batteries returned fire; *Hood* was hit with shell splinters, causing minor damage and injuries to two members of her crew. However, the *Strasbourg* escaped, pursued by *Hood,* and made its way to Vichy France. In the initial bombardment 1,297 French sailors were killed, which apart from neutralising a very real threat, may well, by its ruthlessness and determination, have persuaded General Franco that Spain would be safest remaining neutral and helped convince the United States that Britain was intent on resistance and did not plan to go the way of France and seek an accommodation with the Axis powers.

During the remainder of July and August *Hood* operated with Force H, covering the passage of convoys, attacks on Italian airfields, and escorting carriers flying in Hurricane fighters for the defence of Malta. In August she sailed for Scapa Flow where her service with Force H ended and she resumed duties with the Battle Cruiser Squadron of the Home Fleet. The remaining months of 1940 saw *Hood* at the now-secure Fleet base of Scapa and sailing from there when a heavy ship was needed – for example, in early November when the approaches to Brest and Lorient had to be patrolled in case the German pocket battleship *Admiral Scheer* was headed there after her attack on convoy HX84 and the sinking of the armed merchant cruiser HMS *Jervis Bay*. In fact the *Admiral Scheer* headed south to the Central Atlantic and Caribbean.

In January 1941 *Hood* was docked at Rosyth for refit and for improvements to her radar equipment. By mid-March she was back in service and, with other units of the Home Fleet, attempting to intercept the German battle cruisers *Scharnhorst* and *Gneisenau* on their return from a sortie against Atlantic convoys. Later in March *Hood* was patrolling off Brest, where the German battle cruisers had berthed.

In late April and early May *Hood* was at Hvalfiord, Iceland, to cover convoy routes to the south of Iceland in the event of the breakout of heavy German units. In May *Hood* was at Scapa and on 12 May received the newly appointed Vice Admiral commanding the Battle Cruiser Squadron and Second in Command Home Fleet, Lancelot E. Holland. Intelligence was received that the German battleship *Bismarck* had passed out of the Baltic and had anchored near Bergen, Norway. The *Bismarck,* at 45,000 tons, and capable of high speed and with excellent modern armour protection and mounting eight 15-inch guns, was a formidable threat which could only be matched by a concentration of British forces.

Hood, under Captain Robert Kerr who had assumed command in February, in company with the new, and still untested battleship *Prince of Wales,* sailed for Hvalfiord with a destroyer escort to cover the exit from the Denmark Strait between Iceland and Greenland – one of the most probable routes for *Bismarck* to take. Two cruisers, *Suffolk* and *Norfolk,* were sent into the Denmark Strait and on 23 May sighted *Bismarck* and her consort, the heavy cruiser *Prinz Eugen,* heading for the Atlantic.

Admiral Holland took *Hood* and *Prince of Wales* towards the Strait to cut off the German force. On the face of it the British force, mustering nine 15-inch and ten 14-inch guns, should have been a match for the nine 15-inch and eight 8-inch guns of the German ships. However, *Prince of Wales* was still working up to full efficiency and indeed one of her forward guns was not operational. It had been intended in 1939 to carry out a major reconstruction of HMS *Hood* to improve her armour protection – however, the war had meant that this reconstruction had not been undertaken and she entered her last engagement with protection quite unfitted to resist the German 15-inch shells.

On 24 May *Hood* and *Prince of Wales* approached the German ships from an angle that only allowed their forward gun turrets to bear on the German ships, and for some reason the identity of the German ships was confused and Admiral Holland's initial order was to concentrate fire on the left-hand ship – thinking this was the *Bismarck* – in fact it was the *Prinz Eugen.* The order was corrected but in all probability *Hood*'s few salvos were directed at the lesser target. On board the *Prince of Wales* Admiral Holland's order had been ignored, the gunnery officer correctly identifying *Bismarck* as the right-hand ship. All four ships commenced firing around 5.52am and at 6.00am *Hood* exploded and sank within three or four minutes.

The precise cause of *Hood's* loss has never been entirely established despite Admiralty boards of enquiry. The balance of probability is that a heavy shell from *Bismarck* penetrated armour which had been designed with weight-saving in mind rather than absolute protection, exploded in a magazine and ripped the ship apart. A secondary fire on the upper deck was attributed to shells igniting anti-aircraft rocket ammunition stored there.

The tactical deployment of the two capital ships has been the subject of criticism at the time and since. The Commander in Chief Home Fleet, Admiral Tovey, thought Holland should have allowed the better-protected ship, the *Prince of Wales,* to engage the enemy first and draw his fire away from the more fragile *Hood*. With the loss of *Hood* the German ships concentrated their fire on *Prince of Wales*, which was forced to break off the engagement. Escorting destroyers picked up only three survivors but 1,416 lives were lost on the 'mighty *Hood*' that day.

The sinking of HMS *Hood* was not only an enormous human tragedy, and the loss of a valuable naval unit, but it was also a profound emotional blow to the Royal Navy and to the country at large.

Bismarck evaded her pursuers but having received some damage from shellfire from the *Prince of Wales* the German squadron commander, Admiral Lütjens, decided to make for Brest to refit. A massive gathering of Royal Navy ships was orchestrated to hunt the *Bismarck* and, after attacks from carrier-borne aircraft, she was eventually caught by the battleships *Rodney* and *King George* V on 27 May and reduced to an immobile wreck. Despite enormous damage, the *Bismarck* displayed the legendary endurance of German battleships and remained afloat until torpedoes fired from the cruiser *Dorsetshire* administered the *coup de grâce*. The German battleship sank with the loss of over 2,100 men; 115 survivors were rescued.

Admiral of the Fleet Lord Chatfield (First Sea Lord 1933–8) wrote to *The Times* on 28 May 1941 commenting on their suggestion that *Hood* must have been destroyed by a lucky hit as she was the largest and most powerful ship afloat and had been designed to be invulnerable. After explaining the trade-off that had been made in her design, Chatfield concluded:

The *Hood* was destroyed because she had to fight a ship 22 years more modern than herself. This was not the fault of the British seamen. It was the direct responsibility of those who opposed the rebuilding of the British Battle Fleet until 1937, two years before the second great war started. It is fair to her gallant crew that this should be written.

CHAPTER 14

The *Queen Mary* (1936–) and the Last of the Liners

ON 2 OCTOBER 1942, north of Ireland, Scotland's best-known and best-loved passenger liner, the *Queen Mary*, rammed and sank the anti-aircraft cruiser HMS *Curacoa*. Steaming at almost 30 knots, the 80,000-ton liner struck the escorting cruiser on the port side. In the space of about five minutes *Curacoa* sank, with the loss of 338 officers and men.

A vivid eyewitness account of the disaster was given to a journalist by one of the thousands of American GIs being carried to Britain on board the great liner:

> We assumed she [the cruiser] would change her course and draw alongside, but as she came nearer and nearer it seemed to me that she must inevitably plough directly into our side. Just then, because of the *Queen Mary*'s great length, I lost sight of the cruiser. Seconds later the big liner shuddered perceptibly, but the shock was not sufficient to knock me off my feet. Then we saw the *Curacoa*'s stern, end-up with propellers still turning, and enveloped in thick yellow smoke. We rushed aft along deck and there, off our port stern, was the bow – perhaps two-thirds of her – similarly up-ended, her prow pointing towards the sky. It was also enveloped in smoke and steam. Within five minutes, both sections had disappeared beneath the Atlantic.

At the time of the great ship's launch, the *Mary* had been eulogised in verse by the Poet Laureate, John Masefield, and in a passage of tragic irony he had expressed a hope that she would avoid just such an accident:

> May shipwreck and collision, fog and fire
> Rock, shoal and other evils of the sea
> Be kept from you...

In the darkness, the survivors, pitifully few in number, were brought on board escorting destroyers and the *Queen Mary* limped into the Clyde.

Her bows were badly damaged and only temporary repairs could be effected until her return to New York. A low point in her career had been reached, although intense security meant that few British citizens knew about the incident. When the German propagandist William Joyce (Lord Haw Haw) broadcast this intelligence, his boasting claims were disregarded, as they were in many of the ebbs and flows of the Battle of the Atlantic. The *Queen Mary* was, after all, a vital and irreplaceable keystone of Britain's and, in time, the USA's war-time morale. This ship was part of history – more than that, she made history. She was, and in a sense still is, the quintessential ocean liner, the inevitable or the ultimate ship. Other vessels have had appeal and allure, but none can surpass the *Mary* in these respects, nor can they match her in the variety and interest of her achievements.

First though, we should stress the enormous historical significance of this ship for the people of Scotland and in particular for those who lived on Clydeside. All Clydebuilt ships commanded respect, for they were, in a sense, products of all the people who lived on the river's banks. As mentioned in Chapter 1, the writer Tom Gallacher helped to build the ships and knew them and their owners – the great shipping lines:

> Holt's Blue Funnel with black top ('The Blue Flue'), Donaldson's all black smoke stack, the two red bands ringing the top of the Clan Line, Brocklebank's blue and white bands... they were our ships.

Many other British people had, and still share, this affection for the brand 'Clydebuilt'; for a few examples like the *Mary* this amounted almost to adoration. In a sense the 'ownership' of the *Queen Mary* was vested not in the passengers who paid handsomely for their Atlantic crossings, nor in the company, nor even in the designers, but in the Clydesiders whose skills formed her from blueprint to Queen of the Ocean.

So much for the moment about the myth-making qualities of the *Queen Mary*; what were the practical commercial origins of this icon? Built in the fourth decade of the 20th century, she was a product of an age of competition that to an extent resembled the frenzied arms race that had produced the dreadnought battleships 20 years before. Germany, France and Great Britain now vied with each other for supremacy in a different kind of Atlantic battle and liners like the *Bremen* and the *Normandie* featured in this intense competition. In 1932, the Cunard company (later

FIG. 1

Discovery

After a long career in Polar exploration, including Scott's 1901 expedition to the Antarctic, *Discovery* now forms the central feature of Dundee's Discovery Quay and plays a central role in the city's image.

VisitScotland Angus & Dundee

FIG. J

HMS *Hood* in the Pacific.

An aerial shot of the 'mighty *Hood*' taken when she was on her round the world cruise in 1923/24 as part of the Special Service Squadron. Note the flag of Vice Admiral Sir Frederick Field flying from the mainmast.

US Naval Historical Center

FIG. K

Queen Mary in war-time paint.

The luxury Cunarder in war-time camouflage lying at the Tail of the Bank off Greenock. Notice the fleet of attendant vessels alongside. She has presumably just completed one of her high-speed transatlantic crossings bringing thousands of Allied soldiers to the UK.

Imperial War Museum, A25909

FIG. L

Launch of the puffer *Briton*

The Kirkintilloch shipbuilding yard of J. & J. Hay launched the *Briton* in 1893.
The restricted width of the Forth and Clyde Canal made a side launch rather than the
traditional stern-first launch a necessity.

East Dunbartonshire Libraries

FIG. M

HMS *Vanguard* at high speed.

An impressive view of *Vanguard* steaming at 30 knots on a high speed run during a
NATO exercise in September 1952. *US Naval Historical Centre*

STEAMER "HELENSBURGH," BUILT BY WILLIAM DENNY,

AT DUMBARTON, ABOUT THE YEAR 1826.

FIG. N

Paddle Steamer *Helensburgh*

Built by the renowned Dumbarton shipbuilder William Denny and engined by Robert Napier, *Helensburgh* was one of the fastest steamers of her day.

Authors' Collection

FIG. O

Paddle Steamer *Waverley*

Photographed off Campbeltown, the *Waverley* continues the Clyde steamer tradition of the *Comet* and *Helensburgh*.

Waverley Excursions

FIG. P

Sir Walter Scott

A delightful vintage view of the Loch Katrine steamer *Sir Walter Scott* – named in tribute to the great author's popularisation of the Trossachs area in poems such as 'Lady of the Lake' and novels like *Rob Roy*.

Authors' Collection

FIG. Q

Royal Yacht *Britannia*

Very much the last of a line and a fitting testament to the skills and craftsmanship that made 'Clyde Built' a by-word for quality, even if this product of the Clyde has had to find a final home on the Forth.

Cunard White Star) planned to deliver a knockout punch that would transform this international rivalry. They decided to offer a new fortnightly service shared between two huge speedy ships that would provide a five-day crossing between Southampton and New York and vice versa, doing the job that previously had been done by three ships.

The strategy was agreed – the next Cunard ship to be built would be one that had sufficient speed and size to enable her to cross in five days, allowing for something like an 18-hour turn-round period in port before setting out on the return crossing. This would deliver the new two-ship model, after a second huge liner (eventually to be named the *Queen Elizabeth*) was also planned and built.

If we are to nominate the *Queen Mary* as perhaps the most significant or most dramatic of Scotland's great ships, various considerations about her building should be mentioned. These included interrelated choices and issues such as her size, her design and craftsmanship, her performance, strength and reliability, all of which had decades of experience, tradition, design and engineering lavished on them. John Brown's yard in Clydebank was the one entrusted with the task of addressing these, and other technological issues. The developing narrative of the mighty ship, passing through a brief time of peace and then playing a pivotal role in a great World War – gave the *Mary* her unique status, here and in North America.

The keel was laid in 1930 as No. 534 but shortly after came the Depression, and its dramatic impact upon Clydebank. The most immediate consequence was the suspension of work on building the great ship and consequent mass unemployment.

At this point No. 534 seemed to symbolise the country's economic and industrial plight. In retrospect questions were asked: for example, was it a wise commercial decision, beginning this mammoth enterprise at that particular juncture? Of course, the reasons for commencing the enterprise do not always need to be commercial – other considerations often predominate and among these is the desire for national prestige. This, of course, is a recurrent theme in the story of Scotland's great ships. Sometimes the prestige is embodied in the person of a king or great magnate; one thinks of the personal involvement of James IV and his particular capital ship. However, the prestige that was to be attached to the *Queen Mary* was of a different order altogether. What was at stake for many of the people of Scotland was national pride. For the builders this was mingled with strong corporate identity and ambition, even though there was also a pragmatic realisation that company mergers and other forms of rationalisation would be necessary. Although work on the ship was begun with the niche market of the two-ship service very much in mind – in the end it was kudos not commerce that built the *Queen Mary*. She was, not immediately but ultimately, a nationally subsidised British 'flagship', rather than a commercial winner in an open market.

At any rate the decision was taken to award the contract to John Brown's of Clydebank and, with the highest of hopes on every side, the keel of No. 534 was laid on 1 December 1930 by Cunard's chairman, Sir Percy Bates. The first thousand-foot ship in history, the size compares favourably even with the 21st century's giant cruise ships, and in order to facilitate construction work major adjustments had to be made to the layout of the shipyard – such as the building of temporary rail bridges and so on, necessary in the cramped conditions of John Brown's Clydebank yard on the north bank of the River Clyde.

The keel was completed, but then the ominous economic warnings could be ignored no longer. The workers were warned that they should be ready for 'a reduction in their remuneration'. Why? All ships on the Atlantic run were losing money hand over fist, but this new ship on the stocks was simply eating money. A year, almost to the day from her keel-laying, notices were posted at John Brown's yard gates announcing that work on job No. 534 was suspended. Something approaching 10,000 workers found themselves on the street, as did hundreds from associated companies and suppliers. The hull's steel plating was 80 per cent completed, and the stark skeletal framework of the new ship towered above the surrounding structures for more than two years, watched over by an equally skeletal maintenance force.

A circular was sent by Cunard to shareholders six weeks after the suspension of the building of the 'proposed' No. 534. This made it plain that at that stage the boardroom still viewed the new ship as a strictly commercial item rather than a masterpiece of design and technology or (even) a source of employment.

Your directors are as firmly convinced now as when the orÿer ÿor ÿhe ÿhip was placed that she is the right ship to build as well in the interests of the company as of the nation. They have never lost faith in the company's ability to operate her, either with existing ships or later with a future sister, in such a manner as will enable her to pay her way.

Despite the obvious fact that thousands of Clydeside workers lost their livelihood that day and in the weeks that followed, the directors stuck to their story, that business was business. At the same time the President of the Board of Trade made it plain that there would be no immediate government intervention – this despite the assiduous efforts of concerned public figures like politicians, and especially the indefatigable local MP, David Kirkwood. Therefore the Cunard directors made preparation for the construction of No. 534 by relying on the company's own finances, without government assistance. Harsh economic reality was a priority, even though the announcement referred to the evident pride taken throughout the country in the building of No. 534. The London *Times*, however, reported that the directors were at pains to insist that national prestige was in no sense any part of the basis on which the ship was projected:

> Once such ships become possible they become inevitable… in other words, the fundamental basis of No. 534 is purely economic. That her construction is at this moment suspended depends not on factors inherent in the North Atlantic trade; not on factors domestic to the company, but on international factors [such as the abandonment of the gold standard and the Wall Street Crash] which are hampering the ordinary financial machinery of commerce.

Two more years of hardship for the people of the Clyde passed and the situation began to change significantly. As a result of major restructuring of the shipbuilding industry, No. 534 was now the responsibility of a new merged company, Cunard-White Star Limited, made up of the Cunard Steam Ship Company and the Oceanic Steam Navigation Company. The two fleets were combined as well as other assets. Most importantly, the position had radically changed regarding the intervention of government in the major project of Cunard and John Brown's Shipyard. From now on the unthinkable was a possibility. *The Times* noted:

> In order to provide the requisite finance for the ship No. 534 at Clydebank the Treasury is to make advances not exceeding

£3,000,000 (and) the Treasury will from time to time advance to the merger company sums not exceeding in all £1,500,000 to provide it with the requisite working capital.

The Times' leader on 4 April 1934 ran the headline:

WORK RESTARTED BY 600 MEN, REJOICINGS AT CLYDEBANK

The general conclusion reached by *The Times* leader writer, and by other observers, was that the decision to resume work on the giant vessel, after many rumours and disappointments, could be viewed as a token or symbol of a return to confidence, 'improved conditions and, perhaps, reasonable prosperity'. Slowly realisation dawned on the people of Clydebank that their own prospects were improving. The town had lain under the cold shadow of the giant unfinished structure that for many months had loomed above the slipway running down to the Clyde. Rumours had for so long disappointed the men that they could scarcely believe it when some 600 of them received notices to report for work. Much of the tasks that had to be tackled came under the heading of 'preparatory' but the delight of those selected spread to others not yet started and:

> ... crowds gathered to listen to the horn which marks the beginning and end of periods of labour sound for the first time in nearly 28 months. By half past seven thousands thronged the streets, and the Dalmuir Pipe Band was marching along the road to play the workers in. The men with the admission notes arrived in clean overalls and freshly greased boots, and there were remarkable scenes as they passed through the crowd. Tradesmen still unemployed shook them by the hand and they were greeted with cheering and laughter.

So the work recommenced – the spirit of optimism was not able to withstand all of the difficulties and frustrations of the years that lay ahead, but an additional boost to morale came with the symbolic force of that great ritual of the shipbuilding world, the ship's launch and her naming as *Queen Mary* on 26 September 1934. In a rare entry of the monarch into the public/political arena, King George V commented in his address at the launch:

> For three years her uncompleted hull has lain in silence on the stocks. We know full well what misery a silent dockyard may spread among

a seaport, and with what courage that misery is endured. During those years when work upon her was suspended we grieved for what that suspension meant to thousands of our people. We rejoice that… it has been possible to lift that cloud and to complete this ship.

All aspects of the launch were carefully planned and involved what we now call media hype. In '*Masterpiece in the Making*', a description of the activity in the yard before the launch, we learn that the *Mary* is:

> … exactly the same length as the first hole at Prestwick golf course – 339 yards. And if you could stand her up on end alongside the Eiffel Tower, she would top that structure by 18 feet.

Similar statistics were readily available to the world's press – we learn that the ship was built with 10 million rivets and every single one 'has a man's personality stamped into it'. The Poet Laureate proposed the following valediction for the launch:

> … A rampart of a ship,
> Long as a street and lofty as a tower,[1]

Next, the huge vessel was moved to the fitting out basin and a process began that was once familiar to almost every Clydesider. By September the 27 boilers were lowered into the ship and the engines were installed a year later. Funnels and the ship's masts followed, the myriad finishing tradesmen swarmed all over her and did their transforming work and then she was ready for trials, after an inspection by the new king, Edward VIII.

On her inaugural trip downriver on 24 March 1936, the *Mary* ran aground twice, but with the aid of tugs the journey to Gourock was accomplished. A voyage to her home port of Southampton was successfully completed and then sea trials were carried out. The *Mary* was already perceived as an engineering achievement – now she took on the aura that she has retained even to this day, the aura of celebrity. The ship's decor was subjected to critical judgement and appraisal normally reserved for works of art. Spectacular 'happenings' were planned that promoted the liner's celebrity status. Lord Burghley, the Olympic sprinter and bon viveur, ran a lap of 400 yards on the 724 feet long promenade dock,

---

[1]   Masefield, John, from a poem specially commissioned for the launch of Ship No. 534, in 1936. West Dunbartonshire Libraries

FIG. 14.1
Queen Mary interior – the art deco style of her original design.
Authors' Collection

dressed in full evening clothes. George Blake's report on the maiden trip to New York enthusiastically commented:

> From the bow the impression was of grace and easy speed, a gliding of beauty through the night. ...This was the essential creation of a long line of builders and engineers. Was it too fanciful to imagine that the ghost of Robert Napier hovered there above the spray and the spume, smiling to see his work so superbly perfected?[2]

The maiden transatlantic voyage began on 27 May 1936 and pier 90 in New York Harbour was reached on the first of June. On her sixth trip the *Queen Mary* wrested the Blue Riband for the fastest crossing from the French *Normandie* and, after the war, she did the same to the ss *United States*. A period of successful and popular voyages then followed and the final peacetime crossing from Southampton began on 30 August 1939, arriving in New York the day after war was declared, carrying her largest number of peacetime passengers, 2,552.

---

[2] Blake, George, *Down to the Sea: the romance of the Clyde, its ships and shipbuilders*, HarperCollins Publishers Ltd., London, 1937

FIG. 14.2
Queen Mary converted to a troop-ship.
The crowded accommodation contrasts with pre-war luxury.
Imperial War Museum A25928

Prime Minister Winston Churchill made four wartime crossings of the Atlantic in the *Mary*. Her unmatched speed, and the resulting measure of safety this gave her, was responsible for her unparalleled success as a troop-ship, soon carrying up to 15,000 troops at a time. In a way the ship herself was regarded as a kind of VIP: the fondly regarded liner seemed as much at ease carrying military and political leaders, as previously she had borne film stars and plutocrats in peacetime. For example, she was the setting in 1943 for a series of important planning meetings of Churchill's staff en route to a summit conference with President Franklin D. Roosevelt, to set the date for an Allied invasion of 'Fortress Europe'. Again in 1944 Churchill boarded the 'Grey Ghost' to cross the Atlantic for the Halifax Conference. On these occasions Churchill and his staff maintained a punishing schedule. On the crossings plans were orchestrated for invasion, aerial offensives against Hitler's Germany were discussed and many other strategies associated with the development of war plans were in place before the ship reached its destination.

The *Mary* had been transformed below decks in a remarkable career change. Together with a score or so of other large liners, including her new sister ship the *Queen Elizabeth*, she was converted into a troop ship. The two Queens became the fastest and largest troopships in history.

The *Mary* underwent complete or partial refits on a number of occasions in wartime, to equip her to carry military personnel, first of all Australian and New Zealand forces being transported to the Middle East and the European theatres of war. Most of her service, after the entry of the USA into the war, however, was on the North Atlantic route from New York to Britain, and in particular to Gourock and the Tail of the Bank. From June 1943 these crossings amounted to what could almost be termed a ferry service. She made 28 Atlantic round-crossings in succession, carrying increasing numbers of American GIs together with substantial Canadian forces. A maximum carrying capacity was set at 15,000 troops for summertime crossings, rather less in winter. All in all this was a mass transportation that has not been surpassed, even in post-war years and with the huge cruise ships of today.

Considerable ingenuity was employed in the preparation for the embarkation of troops in the USA. It was treated as a major exercise: complete, full-size, mocked-up, sections of the ship were prepared in New Jersey, and all of the military personnel due to be shipped to Europe, had to carry out a full-blown practice exercise or 'dummy-run'. These practice runs were filmed and embarkation procedures checked and analysed. In order to familiarise the troops with conditions on board the actual ship, the procedures reproduced these circumstances as closely as possible; for example the liner's division into three colour-coded areas, red, white and blue was reproduced in the practice area.

Following such rehearsals, with the troops safely on board, the crossing began. Various tactics were developed that proved extremely successful in safeguarding the ship against submarine or air attacks. There were, for example, shrewd tactics employed by the captain in choosing and setting course. These included the *Mary* zigzagging at speeds of up to 30 knots; at other times she would dispense with her protective screen of warships, when making a dash to elude U-boats.

At the peak of her career, the great liner, packed with troops, was making regular five-day crossings from New York to Great Britain. Disembarking of troops and other personnel accounted for another four days before their being taken by rail on to the South of England, often as part of the build-up for Operation Overlord, D-Day and the opening of the Second Front.

Even then, as the war was entering its closing stages, there was a new job for the *Queen Mary*, because an immense repatriation programme was set in motion. Her return voyage across the Atlantic might involve carrying almost as many troops as on the outward leg; all the more so when the ship began to transport demobilised forces and other categories of passenger, such as war-brides, in vast numbers. All in all, while acting as a troopship, it is reckoned that she carried close to a million GIs and other personnel, and travelled around 600,000 miles.

Proof that the ship's history, even after the war, remained closely linked with the history of her country can be found in the fact that Churchill and his Foreign Secretary Anthony Eden used the *Mary* in 1952 to take them to the USA for talks with President Harry S. Truman. This echo of wartime was part of a process of trying to re-awaken the 'special relationship' with the US that the PM had forged with President Roosevelt.

A few years later still, and a pilot, who often brought the *Queen Mary* into Southampton, gave this evocative view of the *Mary* as she approached the end of her active years of service:

> On the bridge all is hushed; the captain stands near the dimly lighted chart table, the pilot closer to the helmsman, whose ruddy face reflects the glow from the compass before him; the two navigating officers are quiet, ready to help with radar or bearings, alert to any possible danger... The great ship, so solid beneath one's feet, seems scarcely to have engines in her, and it is only by a sort of sixth sense that one knows the propellers are turning at all. One feels a great pride that [the Queens] are ours, and an intense and deeply satisfying desire to help maintain their splendid services... Sometimes I wonder if the era of the great liner is passing. At least the romance, the splendour and perfection of these two ships never will be surpassed.[3]

Just one year after John Radford wrote that description in *Pilot Aboard*, and much sooner than he could have dreamed, the *Queen Mary* took

---

[3] Radford, John, *Pilot Aboard*, Blackwood, London, 1966

her last voyage from Southampton on 31 October 1967. This seriously nostalgic voyage was a true coda to a wonderful career. Rounding Cape Horn for the first (and last) time the *Mary* reached her new home in Long Beach, California on 9 December.

In the same year the Cunard company took something of a gamble in adapting the transatlantic liner concept to a post-war, more versatile role, by launching the QE2 from the same yard as her predecessor. Now, in the 21st century, the former continues with a successful programme based on cruising, as does Cunard's much later *Queen Mary 2*. The difference is that vessels like the *Mary 2* can no longer claim a Clydeside birthplace, and Scots shipbuilders are a dying breed. There is only a handful left of inheritors of the great tradition of skill and craftsmanship that built the *Queen Mary*.

The image on the cover of this book shows a proud workforce and hundreds of spectators at John Brown's Clydebank shipyard at the launch, on 27 September 1967, of the Clyde's last great Cunarder, the QE2. In the 40 years since, she has made periodic returns from the oceans of the world to her birthplace, the most recent in September of 2007. Even then there was no indication that the affection or infatuation that the people of the river has had with this, possibly the last, of Scotland's Great Ships, is coming to an end. The lights of pride and even patriotism burn just as brightly as ever.

On just such an occasion, as the paddler *Waverley* crossed the QE2's wake near the Tail of the Bank, the waving passengers joined with many more spectators on the river's banks. It was as if they were there in celebration of a golden age, or expression of a strong collective will, that refuses to give up an integral part of its maritime heritage.

Strictly speaking, of course, as the years roll on, fewer and fewer of those spectators have any forms of direct employment or family link with the builders and crews of the Great Ships, or indeed any ship. Tom Gallacher's yearnings for 'OUR ships' are no longer valid. The shipbuilding industry has declined that much and the number of employees has shrunk too far. Yet many Scots, not all of them elderly, retain an extraordinary affection for the ships that are the surviving products of the yards; and prompting this affection more than any other ship is the QE2. She is unique now, indeed since she is the only grand passenger ship in our list that remains afloat and working (along with *Waverley* and the real veteran, *Sir Walter Scott*).

QE2 – or Cunard Liner No. 736, as it stated on the invitations to her launch, was built for prestige – her great steam turbine engines were proof of an intention to make her a speedy 'crack' vessel. Certainly, there was an attempt by her designers to latch on to the increasingly lucrative cruise market, but she was described in the specification as a 'liner' – evidence perhaps that they were unwilling to throw away the pre-war mould – and a hankering after Blue Ribands and similar trappings of former days. With the appearance on the scene of the *United States* (1949) and the elegant ss *France* of 1962, there was an expectation that international rivalry would be resumed, and that QE2 would augment the role of the 'Queens' liners, whose careers had been interrupted by war. However, it was soon clear that there could be no return to the halcyon days, as first the *Mary* and then the *Elizabeth* left the stage. That apart, QE2 has certainly enjoyed a far longer and more fruitful career, and is still around long after the French or US rivals also departed the scene.

The Falklands War added an unexpected chapter to the ship's career in 1982, when she served as a troopship on the voyage to the South Atlantic, with a faint echo of the role played by the earlier Queens during the Second World War. For this she underwent a considerable refit that included the installation of three helicopter pads and accommodation for 3,000 troops.

Having successfully completed this hazardous mission an important improvement to QE2 came when she was re-engined (sadly, in Germany not the UK) with a diesel-electric plant that added to her reliability, improved running costs and gave her a new top speed of 34 knots, although increasing emphasis on cruising made that somewhat unnecessary.

The history of cruising over the past 40 years has seen a remarkable evolution and expansion – accompanied by a meteoric rise of air transport and the decline and disappearance of the transatlantic liner – of the cruising industry and of the new gigantic cruise ships like the European-built *Victoria*. The QE2 marked a vital stage in this evolution as a vessel which had the characteristics of a hybrid form – capable of sailing the transatlantic route and of undertaking an extensive cruising programme.

The celebrity passengers – VIPs, film stars, heiresses and sporting gods and goddesses – who had flocked on board the elite liners in the 20s and 30s, would have been astonished at the size and facilities and transformed social and class structure of the QE2, or other typical cruise ships today. Money still talks but essentially most cruise ships – even some of the largest and most garish – are relatively classless. Increasingly these ships have come to resemble giant floating resorts. This impression has been confirmed by the recent announcement that *QE2* will 'retire' from the Cunard fleet in August 2008, for the exotic resort city of Palm Jumeirha, in Dubai, where she will be refitted and then moored (in similar fashion to the *Queen Mary* at Long Beach) as 'a luxury floating hotel, retail, museum and entertainment destination.' In other words: *QE2* will end her days with complete integration into an 'entertainment destination'. But will she still be a ship?

CHAPTER 15

HMS *Vanguard* (1944–60)

WHEN HMS *VANGUARD*, Britain's latest and most powerful battleship, slipped into the Clyde from John Brown's yard at Clydebank on St Andrew's Day 1944, she was already a monument to a vanished age; an age of big gun ships that formed the line of battle and determined the fate of empires. Designed to do a job that, in its essentials, would have been familiar to Nelson at Trafalgar or Jellicoe at Jutland, *Vanguard* had been rendered obsolete by the submarine and by air power. When Princess Elizabeth launched the great ship, Britain was still at war with Germany and Japan. In November 1944 Germany might have been seen to be on her last legs and, with the sinking of her last capital ship, the *Tirpitz*, earlier that month, no longer presented any naval threat to which the *Vanguard*'s 15-inch guns might be a credible response. However, planners envisaged several more years of war in the Far East, and a swift powerful battleship to serve with carrier task groups in the Pacific would be of immense value. Eighteen months' work in fitting-out and testing would elapse, before *Vanguard* was finally accepted into the Royal Navy after sea trials, on 9 August 1946. By this time the war in Europe was long over and the atomic bombs dropped on Hiroshima and Nagasaki in August 1945 had marked the end of the war in the Pacific. *Vanguard* was destined to be a battleship that would never fire her guns in anger.

Britain had entered the Second World War with 15 battleships and battle cruisers, 12 in commission and three undergoing refit. The battle cruiser, as we have seen with HMS *Hood*, was armed similarly to the battleship but attained a higher speed by sacrificing armour protection. Ten of these capital ships of the fleet of 1939 had been ordered before the outbreak of the First World War. Three – the battle cruisers *Hood*, *Renown* and *Repulse* – had been laid down during the First World War and *Renown* and *Repulse* had been completed in time to join the fleet in 1917. Interwar retrenchment and a series of International Naval Treaties had resulted in a decline in the battleship strength of the Royal Navy and as older units were scrapped, new replacement ships were not ordered. The only interwar additions to the battleship fleet that were available in September

1939 were the battleships *Nelson* and *Rodney* – each mounting nine 16-inch guns – the largest calibre guns ever used by the Royal Navy. These two ships were designed to meet the displacement limits laid down in the 1922 Washington Naval Treaty and for reasons of weight reduction, rather than tactical efficiency, had their main armament in three forward-mounted turrets, thus reducing the area where heavy armour plating was required.

British defence planning and procurement between the wars had been predicated on the 10 Year Rule. First laid down in 1919, this stated that, for planning purposes, no major war was to be considered likely in the next 10 years. This rolling period of 10 years continued to limit defence expenditure until it was abandoned in 1932. However, the abandonment of the rule did not immediately result in increased expenditure and no decision to undertake a major re-armament programme was made until 1934.

In the 1936 and 1937 Naval Estimates, provision was made for a new class of fast battleships – the *King George V* class. These ships – *Anson, Duke of York, Howe, King George V* and *Prince of Wales* – were laid down in 1937 and would enter service between 1940 and 1942. HMS *Howe*, built at Fairfield's yard at Govan on the Clyde, demonstrates some of the problems of major warship construction. Priorities changed during the construction and fitting out of the *Howe*, and no matter how badly the Navy wanted a new battleship, other types of ships were often wanted more badly and scarce labour was shifted on to other projects – as we shall see, this also affected *Vanguard*. As a result, although *Howe* was launched in April 1940, it took another 28 months before she was completed.

The ships of the *King George V* class were armed with 10 14-inch guns of a new pattern that were claimed to be more effective and of greater penetrating power than the standard 15-inch guns of British battleships. These guns were arranged in two four-gun turrets fore and aft and a superimposed two-gun turret forward. Despite the advantages of the 14-inch gun, when the *Vanguard* came to be designed and ordered under the War Estimates in 1941 she was to be equipped with eight 15-inch guns arranged in four two-gun turrets – two forward and two aft. These guns already existed in the Admiralty's reserve of weapons and their utilisation saved the very considerable cost of manufacturing new main armament. The disadvantage, pointed out by the First Lord of the Admiralty to the Prime Minister in a September 1942 memo, was that if *Vanguard* lasted 20 years in service her guns would then be nearly 50 years old.

Orders were placed in 1939 for a new class of four battleships, the *Lion* class, from Vickers-Armstrong Barrow, Cammell Laird, John Brown, and Fairfield. These ships were to be approximately 40,000 ton displacement, 781 feet overall and were to be armed with nine 16-inch guns to counter the threat of the heavy German battleships of the *Tirpitz* class. They were planned as an improvement on the *King George V* ships. However, changing perception of needs resulted in the suspension of work on these ships after they had been laid down and a revised plan for one even larger capital ship was prepared by Sir Stanley Goodall, the Director of Naval Construction at the Admiralty.

Vanguard was clearly intended to be bigger and better than any previous British battleship – at 814 feet 4 inches length overall, she was more than 74 feet longer than the KGV class ships. Her designed standard displacement of 42,500 tons was 7,500 tons heavier than the KGVs – approximately the weight of a contemporary cruiser. Her designed speed was at least 29 knots produced by turbine machinery developing 130,000 shaft horsepower against the 110,000 SHP produced by the KGVs.

These qualities were obtained at a high price. *Vanguard* was reported to have cost £9 million, excluding the cost of main armament and mountings, which would have raised the total cost to £11 million. The interwar battleships *Rodney* and *Renown* cost around £7.5 million – all a very far cry from the first modern battleship, HMS *Dreadnought* of 1906, which cost the then enormous sum of £1.79 million.

The rise of air power would affect the role and value of a battleship like *Vanguard* in a variety of ways. The Second World War saw many naval engagements where air power was decisive – even the destruction of the German battleship *Bismarck* by British surface ships had been made possible by the damage inflicted on the *Bismarck* by Swordfish aircraft flying from the carriers *Ark Royal* and *Victorious*. A more bitter lesson was the destruction of Force Z, the new battleship *Prince of Wales* and the battle cruiser *Repulse* operating without air cover, by Japanese aircraft in December 1941. Indeed, of the five British capital ships lost during the Second World War only one, HMS *Hood*, was sunk by enemy surface craft. The other two, *Royal Oak* and *Barham*, were torpedoed by submarines.

The war in the Pacific had shown that the core of the fleet was now the large aircraft carrier and the battleship was reduced to a protective role for carrier task forces and convoys and as a mobile shore bombardment unit. Some of the decisive battles of the Pacific War, such as Midway in June 1942, had been fought without any of the combatants coming within gun range and with all the attacks being carried out by carrier-borne aircraft. Closer to home, the attack on the Italian fleet at Taranto in November 1940 by 21 Swordfish aircraft flying from HMS *Illustrious* had demonstrated the effectiveness of even a modest amount of air power at sea.

For many years large ships – battleships, battle cruisers and cruisers – had carried one or more catapult-launched aircraft for reconnaissance and gunnery spotting duties. As originally designed, *Vanguard* would have carried such aircraft. However, in the new age of air power she would normally operate as part of a task group with aircraft carriers and there was less need for her own onboard aircraft, the advent of early-warning and gunnery-spotting radar also diminished the need for a battleship to carry reconnaissance and spotting aircraft. At a fairly advanced stage in construction the decision was taken to delete the aircraft and catapult and to utilise the space for the provision of additional anti-aircraft guns.

These and other changes caused delay, and progress on building the giant ship was soon causing concern. The First Lord of the Admiralty, A. V. Alexander, the Cabinet Minister responsible for the Navy, wrote to Winston Churchill, Prime Minister and Minister of Defence, on 24 September 1942, presumably in a response to one of Churchill's enquiries, that there was no firm date available for completion. He also volunteered the information that a committee at the Admiralty had been considering the possibility of converting the *Vanguard*'s hull into an armoured aircraft carrier, so providing an additional *Ark Royal* class carrier at an earlier date than the ships of that class currently building. Such a conversion was not a new idea; in the First World War cruisers, a battleship and a passenger liner had been converted into aircraft carriers.

Churchill, who had been First Lord of the Admiralty from September 1939 to May 1940, observed that this proposal was new to him. Vice Admiral William F. Wake-Walker, Third Sea Lord and Controller of the Navy, the officer responsible for warship construction, reported that if the decision to convert was taken within the month *Vanguard* could be in service as a carrier by early 1946. The First Sea Lord, Admiral of the Fleet Sir Dudley Pound, the professional head of the Navy, minuted that fast capital ships were needed to support carriers in the Pacific, in invasions and on the convoys to Russia and that air power could be effectively delivered from the intermediate-sized carriers. As *Vanguard* should be ready as a battleship sooner than as a carrier, the original plan should be adhered to.

The main difficulty in construction of *Vanguard* was not, however, an extravagant plan to redesign her as a carrier, or alterations to her equipment. It was simply that there was insufficient capacity in John Brown's yard to handle all the work on hand – a situation that was reflected in every British shipyard. The construction of large warships could only be carried out by a relatively small number of shipyards. The six battleships and the 12 largest aircraft carriers constructed during the war came from only seven major yards such as John Brown's and Fairfield on the Clyde (two each), Harland and Wolf in Belfast (four carriers) and Cammell, Laird in Birkenhead, the *Prince of Wales* and *Ark Royal*. These yards were immensely pressured by the demands of war. Large-scale projects tied up a building berth at these yards for long periods and demanded large numbers of skilled workers. The vast expansion of the wartime navy, the need to repair and refit war-damaged ships, and the need to replace sunk merchant shipping, all meant that shipyard space was under great pressure. In September 1942 it was noted that, apart from *Vanguard*, the Clydebank yard had seven destroyers building as well as the fleet aircraft carrier *Indefatigable,* the auxiliary carrier *Nairana,* and the cruiser *Bellerophon.* All merchant ship construction at the yard had been stopped in December 1941. Work had been suspended on *Bellerophon* in January 1942 to allow progress to be made on *Vanguard* and as *Indefatigable* moved towards completion the yard's intention was to transfer labour to work on the *Vanguard.*

The complexities of the situation were considerable. *Indefatigable* had to be launched by December 1942 or the tides would not serve for the launch of such a large ship in the narrow waters of the Upper Clyde until March 1943 – so work had to be accelerated on her to meet these constraints. Progress was, however, dependent on having workers and even with wartime regulations on the direction of labour, John Brown's was experiencing a severe skills shortage – in November 1942 the Controller of the Navy reported that the yard was short of 500 men and 150 women and that they actually had 60 fewer employees than in May 1942. Trade Union restrictions on interchangeability of labour were exacerbating the problem.

In December 1942 Churchill even raised the possibility of total cancellation of *Vanguard*. Writing to the First Lord, he said:

If she is not to be fit for service till March 31 1946 the whole question of her future construction must be reviewed.[1]

When Sir Andrew Cunningham succeeded Pound as First Sea Lord in October 1943, he formed the opinion that *Vanguard* was a waste of money and resources as he was sure she could not be completed in time for the campaign against Japan. However, too much had been spent to make cancellation an option.

Nevertheless, even the longest construction period eventually ends, and on 2 May 1946 *Vanguard* steamed down the Clyde from John Brown's fitting-out basin to the Tail of the Bank for preliminary trials. These continued through June and July, leading to her final acceptance by the Navy on 9 August 1946.

By 1946 the Navy was reducing its forces in the light of the reduced threat, changed technologies and post-war economic difficulties. Between the end of the war and 1950, 10 battleships and battle cruisers were consigned to the scrapyard. The remaining battleship force consisted of the four surviving *King George V* class ships and *Vanguard*.

Vanguard's first major employment came in 1947 when she took King George VI, Queen Elizabeth and the Princesses Elizabeth and Margaret on a Royal Tour to South Africa. *Vanguard* had been praised in the press when she was under trials for the attention which had been paid to the crew's comfort – as *The Times* noted:

> She will have the most comfortable mess-deck in the Royal Navy, and many of the amenities of a luxury liner are incorporated in her equipment. The plastic cups, plates and dishes used on the mess-decks are cleaned by machinery.

However, even the accommodation designed for an Admiral and his staff, when used to house the Royal Family, was thought to require modification – and the dockyard costs for fitting up *Vanguard* for the Royal trip came to £169,129.

Following this tour, *Vanguard* settled down to a peacetime existence, serving at various times as the Flagship of the Training Squadron, the Home Fleet and the Mediterranean Fleet. The only conflict in which she might have been employed was the Korean War (1950–3), and although

---

[1] National Archives ADM1/12127

Royal Navy carriers, cruisers and destroyers were deployed to the area the remaining battleships were not used in the theatre.

A problem was identified with *Vanguard* at an early date – due to the extra equipment with which she was fitted her structure was overstressed and her ship's books instructed that, except in emergencies, she should not operate at more than 35 foot draught. This was normally achieved by reducing the amount of bunker fuel carried.

In 1952 a plan to use *Vanguard* to take the King, for the sake of his health, on a cruise to South Africa and for a stay at Botha House, Natal, the official residence of the Prime Minister of South Africa, had been prepared and *Vanguard* was scheduled to leave Portsmouth on 8 March. However, the King's condition worsened and he died of lung cancer on 6 February.

In exercises in 1955 *Vanguard's* 15-inch guns were fired for the last time, and in 1956 she was transferred to the Operational Reserve and became Flagship of the Reserve Fleet and an accommodation vessel. The late 1950s saw the battleship force dwindle with *Anson* being scrapped in 1957, and *Duke of York*, *Howe* and *King George V* going to breaker's yards at Faslane and Dalmuir in 1958.

In January 1960 the Admiralty authorised the disposal of *Vanguard*. There were objections to the loss of the country's last battleship and proposals were made that she should be preserved, like HMS *Victory*, as a national monument. Realism prevailed – preservation would require either a dedicated dry-dock or by maintenance afloat with unacceptably high costs for annual upkeep. As an Admiralty official minuted, *Vanguard* was 'a lovely ship and an outstanding feat of Naval Architecture'[2] but she was hardly as historically significant as Nelson's flagship.

The White Ensign was hauled down for the last time at sunset on 7 June and on 4 August she started her final voyage, under tow, for her appointment with the ship breakers at Faslane, on the Gareloch, 20 miles from her birthplace at Clydebank. On leaving Portsmouth she ran aground and for several hours the Isle of Wight ferries were suspended as efforts were made to refloat her. Eventually the last of the long line of British battleships was freed from the mud and continued on her way to her destruction.

The line of modern battleships is generally considered to have started

---

[2] National Archives ADM1/27480

FIG. 15.1
HMS *Vanguard* at sea.
Britain's last battleship photographed from the deck
of a British aircraft carrier.

US Naval Historical Center

with *Dreadnought* in 1906, although its roots go back to ships like *Black Prince*. *Vanguard* was the end of this line of famous names and great ships, and in many ways the most powerful and arguably the most handsome of the line. She was, however, overtaken by changed technologies and new patterns of warfare which had effectively made even the most powerful and effective battleship obsolete, just as the *Dreadnought* had made earlier capital ships redundant half a century earlier.

CHAPTER 16

PS *Waverley* (1947–)

WHEN THE LONDON and North Eastern Railway commissioned a new paddle steamer for their service from Craigendoran to Arrochar, they certainly had no idea that the ship they ordered from A. & J. Inglis of Pointhouse, Glasgow, would 60 years later be the last sea-going paddle steamer in the world.

The paddle steamer was in 1947 a rather dated concept, but the LNER operating from the restricted depth of Craigendoran on the north bank of the River Clyde near Helensburgh, had stuck to the traditional paddle steamer and its advantage of shallow draught, when other companies had adopted screw propulsion and, in some cases turbine engines. The *Waverley*, 239.6 foot long, 693 gross tonnage, would be – though much larger, more powerful and technically more advanced – the lineal descendant of Henry Bell's *Comet* of 1812 (see Chapter 5). Like the *Comet*, the new ship would cater for two markets. The first was the essential communication

FIG. 16.1
Waverley
The last sea-going paddle steamer.
Waverley Excursions

link between the Loch Long and Loch Goil communities and the railhead at Craigendoran, while the second was the demand for pleasure sailing. In the environment of post-war austerity and shortages that prevailed in 1945 when the order was placed with Inglis, it is extremely unlikely that scarce resources would have been devoted to a ship designed solely for the tourist trade, but the regular service of passengers to these communities warranted the building of a new ship.

The LNER had lost two ships during the Second World War; both had been requisitioned for service as minesweepers. *Marmion* was sunk in an air attack off Harwich in April 1941 and an earlier *Waverley,* the third steamer of that name to sail on the Clyde, was lost at Dunkirk in May 1940 in the effort to evacuate the men of the British Expeditionary Force.

This earlier *Waverley* had been built in 1899 for the North British Steam Packet Company, a subsidiary of the North British Railway. The merger of railway companies in 1923 saw the North British fleet transfer to the LNER. The North British ship names were inspired by the works of Sir Walter Scott – a custom retained by the LNER with ships such as the *Jeanie Deans* (1931) and the unique diesel electric paddle steamer *Talisman* (1935).

Like her 1947 successor, the 1899 *Waverley* had been built by Inglis and had been used as an excursion steamer. She had been called up for service with the Royal Navy as a minesweeper in the 1914–18 war and had returned to the Clyde and her programme of excursion sailings. In 1939 she again wore the White Ensign until she was bombed at Dunkirk.

The Clyde in the first years of the 20th century was so very different from even the post-Second World War river, let alone that of today, that it is worth a brief glance at the complex pattern of services and competing companies. In the last year of peace, 1914, there were six steamers of the North British Railway, including *Waverley* operating services from Craigendoran. Across the Clyde, ships of the Caledonian Steampacket Company ran from Gourock and Wemyss Bay, while the Ayrshire coast ports were the home to nine ships of the Glasgow and South Western Railway. Four modern turbine-powered steamers owned by Turbine Steamers Ltd competed with the railway companies, as did four ships owned by Buchanan Steamers Ltd, three owned by John Williamson, as well as two providing services between Glasgow and Campbeltown operated by the Glasgow & Campbeltown Steampacket Co. Three fine ships – *Iona*, *Columba* and *Grenadier* – of David MacBrayne linked the Clyde with the Loch Fyne ports while Loch Long was also served by Cameron's *Lady Rowena* – in all, a staggering total of 40 passenger ships operating on the Clyde.

The Clyde was a very competitive arena for ships, with intense rivalry between the competing companies – a rivalry that at times resulted in ships racing each other to be first at the next pier, an activity which had more than one steamer skipper appearing in court on charges of reckless behaviour. It was also a centre from which ships, after a career on the river and firth, found their way to other less demanding settings. The novelist Neil Munro, writing in his delightful 1907 travel book *The Clyde, River and Firth* expressed this tendency as follows:

> Clyde ships, second-hand, grown obsolete for Glasgow passengers, go, at the end, to less fastidious quarters, so that 'crocks' from the Clyde have glorified the lower Thames and provided a standard of elegance for the traveller to Clacton and Southend; and elsewhere in English waters the Scotsman often comes upon old friends of the 'Fair' holidays working under aliases. Such good stuff are those old Clyde passenger steamers that they seem immortal, and their owners buff out the natal dates on their bells and engine brasses, ashamed, perhaps, to be found demanding the labour of youth from such veterans.[1]

This migration of steamers from the Clyde to other routes had been a significant feature of the river from the earliest days of steam. The *Margery*, launched in June 1814 at the Dumbarton shipyard of William Denny, was sold off the river in November of that year and sailed, via the Forth and Clyde Canal and the East Coast route, to take up a new career on the Thames, later crossing to France to go into passenger service on the Seine as the *Elise*. Even more striking was the sale of the Port Glasgow-built *Argyll* to London owners in May 1815. Not content with sailing the 72-foot long ship down to the Thames by the longer and more exposed West Coast route, the new management decided to sell tickets for the journey – almost certainly the world's first ocean steamship cruise. The advertisement in the Glasgow newspapers explained all:

---

[1] Munro, Neil, *The Clyde, River and Firth*, A&C Black, London, 1907

Marine Excursion from the Clyde to the Thames

A select party, not exceeding six, may be accommodated in the *Thames* schooner, late the *Argyll* steam engine packet. The vessel has received many improvements, is perfectly seaworthy, and enabled to proceed either by steam or sails, separately or united.

Those wishing to enjoy this novel and interesting trip along the Coast of Scotland, Wales and Ireland, will please apply to William Kerr, the Agent, Broomielaw.

Isaac Weld, who with his wife joined the *Thames* when she put into Dublin for repairs, wrote a fascinating account of the voyage. The steamship attracted huge crowds at every port she put into and alarmed the fishermen on the Cornish coast who, sighting this strange vessel moving without the benefit of sails and spewing out smoke and flames, were convinced that she was a sea devil.

FIG. 16.2
Steamers at Glasgow
A characteristic view of steamers at the Broomielaw.
The left-hand ship is the *Ivanhoe*.
Authors' Collection

Almost 50 years later Clyde paddle steamers were still in demand, this time as blockade runners for the Confederate States of America. When the war between the Northern and Southern states broke out in 1861 the Federal Navy imposed a blockade on the ports of the Confederacy. The South, a largely agricultural area, needed to export its principal cash crop, cotton, and import manufactured products and munitions to enable the war to be carried on.

The shallow-draught Clyde paddle steamer – fast, manoeuvrable and low in profile – was an ideal vessel for the blockade running role and Confederate agents were soon seen around the Clyde ordering ships from yards such as William Denny at Dumbarton and J. & G. Thomson at Govan. In the urgency of war they were unable to wait for ships to be built and bought, at premium prices, ships that were already in service on the river. Ships such as the *Eagle* (1852), *Gem* (1854), *Jupiter* (1856), *Kelpie* (1857), *Spunkie* (1857), *Pearl* (1859), *Ruby* (1859), *Juno* (1860) and *Neptune* (1860) were bought in secret deals and slipped out of the Clyde for undisclosed destinations.

Perhaps the most famous such purchase was the paddle steamer *Iona* – built in 1855 by Thomsons and operated by David Hutcheson & Co. on the long run from Glasgow to Ardrishaig, a route where her 17 knot speed was a desirable asset. It also made her a prime target for Confederate agents and *The Times* of Thursday 18 September 1862 carried a report from the *North British Daily Mail*:

> The favourite and crack steamer *Iona* was withdrawn from her station between Glasgow and Ardrishaig on Monday last, the beautiful saloon steamer *Fairy* taking her place. We are told that this withdrawal is caused by the *Iona* having been sold to the Confederates in America. It is also rumoured that the fine Belfast paddle steamer *Giraffe* and the West Highland steamer *Clydesdale* have also been disposed of to the same parties. If this be true, then the very flower of our Clyde passenger steamers will have been withdrawn to make room, it is hoped, for others equal at least, if not superior, to those we shall have lost. The *Iona* is a steamer of world-wide fame. She has carried thousands upon thousands of passengers over the famed Royal route for years, many of them from the most remote parts of the globe; and, go where she will, she will maintain the character of our Clyde builders and engineers.

In the event *Iona* was never to reach her destination. After the necessary preparations for an Atlantic crossing and her normal livery being covered over with grey paint she slipped downriver on 2 October, bound for Nassau in the Bahamas, a noted base for the blockade runners. Off Gourock she paused to adjust her compasses and was run into by a new steamer, *Chanticleer*, returning from her trial trip. *The Times* reported as follows:

> The *Chanticleer* first grazed with her starboard the right paddle-box of the *Iona*, then struck her about a dozen feet nearer the stern, carrying away her after funnel and mainmast, and cutting her right through the centre, to within two feet of her left side. The collision took place at 10 minutes past 7, and the two vessels remained in contact for half an hour, hanging to each other. It was apparent, however, from the damage done to the *Iona* that she would soon sink. Accordingly the whole of the crew were removed to the *Chanticleer*, and the two vessels were then separated. Not long afterwards the *Iona* went down in water 150 feet deep. She was heavily laden with stores for the Confederate Government. The damage done to the *Chanticleer* was inconsiderable.

From the earliest days of Clyde steamers, they had been more than workaday vessels designed to be efficient passenger transports – the steamer, as we have seen when considering the *Comet*, did much to create the tourist industry. As early as 1815 the owners of the *Greenock* steamer advertised a special autumn sailing to Inveraray, pointing out that:

> ... the scenery of the Clyde, the Kyles of Bute and Lochfine, are excelled by none in Europe. It is particularly grand at this time of the year, and the beauties and grandeurs of Inveraray Castle, the Pleasure Grounds and Deer Park exceed description, and all respectable visitors are allowed to see the whole.

A few years later a Greenock firm wrote to a Highland landowner: 'There exists here and Glasgow, we may call it a fanaticism for steam boat excursions in summer'. Mass tourism had arrived.

It may, in 1815, have been a reasonably select form of mass tourism, but as the century advanced Glasgow and the West of Scotland started what can only be described as a collective love affair with the steamers.

The performance of steamers and the idiosyncrasies of their skippers were a commonplace of conversation and the custom of going 'doon the watter' became entrenched in the Glasgow mind. A local writer, Bass Kennedy, writing verse in the 1880s, expressed the sentiment well. He puts the following lines in the mouth of a Bridgeton weaver:

> Come listen tae me, Nannie dear,
> My cantie, tosh aul' wife,
> We've stood for five and thirty years
> The tussel an' the strife.
> An' yearly as the time cam' roun',
> We never missed, I'm shair,
> Tae spen' oor sair-won pastime doon
> The watter at the Fair.
>
> Ye min' yon July morn langsyne,
> A rosy morn like this,
> You pledged tae be for ever mine,
> An' sealed it wi' a kiss.
> On board the *Petrel,* near Dunoon,
> Ye yielded tae my prayer,
> An' aye sin' syne we've managed doon
> The watter at the Fair.

The poem ends with the thought:

> A twalmonth's toil in Glesca toun
> Is lichtsome, I declare,
> Wi' twa-three days' diversion doon
> The watter at the Fair.[2]

The *Petrel,* on whose deck the weaver and his lass plighted their troth, enjoyed 40 years of service on the Clyde between 1845 and 1885. She followed another steamer, the *Emperor,* into the controversial area of Sunday sailings. When the *Emperor* first started to sail on a Sunday in 1853 she caused civil disturbance and breach of the peace when she

---

[2] Kennedy, Bass, *Doon the Watter at the Fair* quoted in Osborne, Brian D & Armstrong, *Mungo's City, a Glasgow Anthology,* Birlinn, Edinburgh, 1999

FIG. 16.3
The pioneering turbine steamer *King Edward.*
Argyll & Bute Libraries

attempted to land her passengers at Garelochhead pier. This call was very much against the wishes of the pier's proprietor, Sir James Colquhoun of Luss, who mustered his estate workers to defend the sanctity of the Scottish Sabbath. Curiously enough the requirement on the estate workers to give up their day of divinely ordained rest did not seem to strike anyone as hypocritical or inconsistent.

The Sabbath-breaking *Emperor* had not added to its offence by selling alcohol on board (although passengers may well have carried drink on board). Licensing laws prohibited the sale of alcohol on a Sunday to all except bona fide travellers, but ships were not covered by the provisions of the licensing law, and working class passengers, enjoying a sail 'doon the watter' on a Sunday enjoyed the facility to drink – a market which the *Petrel* was to exploit with some success.

So considerable was the feeling against the drunken and disorderly behaviour on Clyde steamers that the Firth of Clyde Steam Packet Company in 1880 put a new steamer, *Ivanhoe,* into service with the unique selling proposition that she was a temperance ship. This catered for both the more genteel passenger who did not wish to mix with a drunken crowd of the lower orders, and to the considerable working class temperance movement of the time. *Ivanhoe* was a considerable success but her career as a 'dry' ship ended in 1897 when she was purchased by the Caledonian Steam Packet Company, and swiftly commenced the sale of alcohol.

The fourth and present *Waverley* made her maiden trip on Monday 16 June 1947 and sailed from Craigendoran for Arrochar and restored the classic LNER 'Three Lochs Tour', which had been in abeyance since the outbreak of war in 1939. Two of the lochs – Loch Goil and Loch Long – were traversed by the *Waverley* on her way to Arrochar, where passengers could disembark and be transported across to Tarbet on Loch Lomond where one of the two Loch Lomond steamers, *Prince Edward* and *Princess May*, awaited to take them to Balloch at the southern end of the loch.

The arrival of the *Waverley* brought the LNER Craigendoran fleet up to four ships, still one fewer than in the pre-war period. Her companions were the diesel electric paddler *Talisman*, *Jeanie Deans* and the veteran *Lucy Ashton*, which had been built in 1888 at Rutherglen and had still a couple of years of service left before the scrapyard called. In fact, *Lucy Ashton* would have a second life as the test bed for jet-propelled experimental work carried out by the British Shipbuilding Research Association. A normally powered vessel converts energy to thrust through propellers or paddles and inevitable losses ensue. The *Lucy Ashton*'s hull was fitted with four Rolls Royce Derwent jet engines and carried out a variety of test runs in the Clyde and Gareloch, a somewhat noisier method of propulsion than local residents were used to.

The captain of the *Waverley* when she entered service was J. E. Cameron, who had served as navigating officer on the previous *Waverley* at Dunkirk and had later commanded minesweepers in the Mediterranean. In the June 1945 King's Birthday Honours List, Acting Temporary Lieutenant Commander John Ewen Cameron RNR was awarded the Distinguished Service Cross for his wartime services.

In 1948 the railway companies and their associated shipping interests were nationalised and *Waverley* and her sister ships were transferred to the ownership of the British Transport Commission, and then in 1951 to the Caledonian Steam Packet Company. In 1971 this merged with the West Highland shipping company David MacBrayne to form Caledonian

MacBrayne. In 1956/57 *Waverley* was converted from a coal-burning ship to an oil-fired one – an end to the smut and smoke of the classic steamer. By 1971 the whole world of the Clyde steamer was clearly ending. Of *Waverley's* ex-LNER stablemates the *Lucy* had long gone, the *Talisman* was broken up in 1967 and the *Jeanie Deans* had been sold off the river in 1966. New small motor vessels – *Maid of Ashton, Maid of Argyll, Maid of Cumbrae* and *Maid of Skelmorlie* – replaced the paddlers and turbine ships and car ferries began to play a more significant role in Clyde services.

By 1973 Caledonian MacBrayne could see no commercial future for the *Waverley* but agreed to sell her for a nominal consideration of £1 to the Paddle Steamer Preservation Society – the Society's ambitions were, however, much more extensive than just the preservation of the *Waverley* as a static museum exhibit, and the Waverley Steam Navigation Company was created to operate the ship.

Since then, *Waverley* has cruised the waters of the Clyde for which she was designed, and as if to prove the truth of the 'sea-going' boast, has gone forth from Scotland to delight passengers and earn income in cruising such distant waters as the Bristol Channel, the English Channel and the Thames.

Clyde-built implies quality and reliability, but not even Clyde-built ships are immortal and *Waverley* underwent a £7million pound refit ending

FIG. 16.4
An earlier *Waverley* – an early photograph of *Waverley III.*
Authors' Collection

in 2003 which should ensure a long and successful future for this remarkable link with the Clyde's past.

An even more remarkable survivor than the *Waverley* is the Loch Katrine steamer *Sir Walter Scott*. This veteran first sailed in 1900 and was built, at a cost of £4,250, by the Dumbarton shipyard of William Denny and Brothers, with engines by the Dumbarton firm of Matthew Paul & Co. The 110-foot long, 115-ton steel screw steamer was prefabricated at Dumbarton, shipped in sections on a barge up the River Leven and Loch Lomond, and carried by horse and cart over the hill from Inversnaid on Loch Lomondside to Stronachlachar on Loch Katrine, where she was reassembled in the heart of the Trossachs, an area whose tourist potential had been brought to an international audience by Walter Scott in poems such as *Lady of the Lake* and his novels *Waverley* and *Rob Roy*. Hardly surprising, then, that the two earlier Loch Katrine steamers had been named *Rob Roy* nor that their replacement should commemorate the great Scottish writer.

At one time, of course, all the major Scottish freshwater lochs boasted regular services – such as the *Fairy Queen* on Loch Eck, the *Countess of Breadalbane* on Loch Awe and, of course, Loch Lomond with up to four steamers in service in the interwar years.

The *Sir Walter Scott* is now owned by Scottish Water and operated by a charitable trust. Her future was assured in 2005 by a Scottish Executive grant to cover emergency repairs and the operating deficit. Although motorship sailings are still provided on, for example, Loch Etive and Loch Awe, and the restoration of the Loch Lomond paddle steamer *Maid of the Loch* is underway, there is certainly nothing on Scotland's inland waters to equal the experience of cruising on Loch Katrine propelled by the original 20 horsepower triple expansion engines of this elegant centenarian.

CHAPTER 17

RY *Britannia* (1953–)

IN THE GLORIOUS SUMMER of 2006, HM Queen Elizabeth II proposed to take a party of invited guests on a summer cruise of the Hebrides. Such an excursion often formed part of the annual retreat to Balmoral, that fixture in every British monarch's summer holiday since the days of Queen Victoria. The trouble was that *Britannia*, the last of the Royal Yachts, was not available to the Queen – afloat for a little longer, but no longer available to Her Majesty.

The story had caused a stir in the ranks of the media's vigilant pack of royal-watchers and brought her Scottish subjects some considerable pleasure too; the jocular headlines told it all:

BALMORAL-ON-SEA: CRUISE WITH THE QUEEN

The news had broken that as a special celebration in the Queen's 80th year she was chartering the *Hebridean Princess*, a former car ferry built for Caledonian MacBrayne in 1964 for the Oban-Craignure-Lochaline service. Originally named *Columba* and now in lavish form and finish and scarcely makeshift, she is refitted as a luxury cruise ship, run by Hebridean Island Cruises, part of a tourist package much favoured by wealthy visitors to Scotland. The *Hebridean Princess* carries around 50 passengers in a similar number of state rooms – this vessel, stubby but truly Hebridean in character, was selected by the Queen as a temporary replacement for her former royal yacht *Britannia*. She also had a strong Scottish connection, having been built by John Brown of Clydebank. *Britannia*, after being taken out of service in December 1997, has, since 1998, been moored at the Port of Leith and open to the public as a much-admired and integral part of the Ocean Terminal development.

The history of royal yachts and similar ships of state is an intriguing one; in a sense, all ships of the King's or the Queen's Navy can be viewed as personal possessions and one can trace the connection with Scottish and British monarchs' fondness for their own prestige vessels right down from Robert the Bruce's 'gret schip' in the River Leven. Some of the Hebridean

FIG. 17.1
Royal Yacht *Britannia* – dining room.
Royal Yacht Britannia

galleys and birlinns were impressive ships of state – in addition, of course, these were probably shock attack weapons as well as 'showboats' or extensions of the ruler's properties and prestige. This was certainly true of the Stewart monarchs' naval ships that operated on several occasions against rebellious elements in the Hebrides, quite often from a strategic base at Dumbarton. In particular, it is possible to view James IV's great warship, the *Michael* (see Chapter 3), as a forerunner of the royal yacht per se, as he boasted of that mould-breaking symbol of prestige and virility to his royal contemporaries.

Nearer our own day, there was some competition between Britain and other powers: US presidents had little-used official yachts and in the 19th and 20th centuries Prussian kings and German emperors set a cracking pace in a rivalry that at times bore a resemblance to the *Dreadnought*-inspired arms race.

An important step taken in the (still polite) rivalry between these two expansionist powers could be seen in 1878 with the launch of the royal steam yacht *Hohenzollern* – the pride and joy of Kaiser Wilhelm II, who happened to be a grandson of Queen Victoria. His ocean-going yacht, at 4,500 tons and driven by twin-screws, with engines of 9,000 horsepower, was larger and faster than many transatlantic steamers of the day. The traditional emphasis in Prussian strategic thinking had been, since the days of Frederick the Great, on land armies, but, like the British Imperial strategists, Wilhelm II also favoured ships and sea power as expressions of the national will. The *Hohenzollern* with the Kaiser on board, accompanied by a crack battle squadron, visited Great Britain in the summer of 1889 to take part in a grand Anglo-German naval review at Spithead. The *Hohenzollern* was met near the Nab lightship by the Prince of Wales on board the much smaller British royal yacht HMY *Osborne*. They steamed side by side past the arrayed British fleet and came ashore at East Cowes, where Wilhelm paid a formal visit to his grandmother, who bestowed on him the rank of Admiral of the Fleet.

Queen Victoria enjoyed the use of a number of vessels, including three successive HMYs, *Victoria & Albert*, the third of which served no fewer than four monarchs, and survived until after the Second World War, when a decision was finally made to replace her.

Most of the earlier royal yachts were built south of the border but several of them ventured into Scottish waters. Such excursions attracted much public attention and pictorial records of them include the splendid large painting (by Hope J. Stewart) that hangs in West Dumbartonshire Council Offices, showing HMY *Fairy* on a cruise to Scotland. This attractive little yacht is seen at Dumbarton Rock on the occasion of Queen Victoria's visit in 1847 when she accepted the keys of the Royal Castle. When the royal yachts were not available to make such cruises other vessels were chartered instead, as in the case of the *Hebridean Princess* of today. These stand-ins have included warships, such as HMS *Surprise*, a despatch vessel for the Commander-in-Chief Mediterranean Fleet, which served this function in the early 50s and, in particular, stood in for the not-quite-finished *Britannia* at the Coronation Fleet Review off Spithead on 15 June 1953.

Britannia was built at the shipyard of John Brown & Co. Ltd in Clydebank, launched by the Queen on 16 April 1953 and commissioned on 11 January 1954. The cost was an impressive £2,098,000 and *Britannia* gave 44 years of service, comparing favourably with the half century recorded by her predecessor *Victoria & Albert*. Some thought that Clydebank won the contract to build her because of memories of the serious mishap that had occurred following the launch in 1899 of the *V&A* when the latter had almost capsized. Certainly, Queen Victoria had kept her vow never to step on board the *V&A*, and this may have influenced the choice of a shipyard on the Clyde to be the new yacht's builder. The ship's design does make allowance for a sense of continuity and details such as the inclusion of the wheel from George V's racing yacht and the binnacle taken from the *Royal George* of 1817 are evidence of that.

During *Britannia's* career as Royal Yacht (she was designed to be converted into a hospital ship in time of war, though this facility was never used), she conveyed the Queen, other members of the Royal Family, and various dignitaries on 696 foreign visits and 272 visits in British waters. The ship was also intended to serve as a mobile refuge for the British Royal Family in the event of nuclear warfare with the Soviet Union. The state apartments, which are now available for special functions, were designed to accommodate up to 250 guests. The present Prince of Wales and Princess Diana took a honeymoon cruise aboard her in 1981.

Britannia also evacuated over 1,000 refugees from the civil war in Aden in 1986. The Royal Yacht's last foreign mission formed part of an eight-month voyage incorporating 28 visits to 18 countries; she was also to convey the last British governor of Hong Kong, Chris Patten, and Prince Charles, away from Hong Kong after the return of the British colony to the People's Republic of China on 1 July 1997. HMY *Britannia* was decommissioned on 11 December 1997, after a unique Paying Off ceremony and Thanksgiving service followed by Beating the Retreat. She is now known simply as *Britannia*.

She was one of the last fully riveted ships to be built and the exacting standards of the designers can be seen in the steps that were taken to ensure a smooth finish on the hull. In the end the rivets were countersunk into the steel plates and then the rivet heads were chamfered off and painted, giving the hull its wonderful finish. Such attention to detail was characteristic of *Britannia* throughout. In particular, the interior, designed by Sir Lewis Casson, is a masterpiece of British design, influenced by the Festival of Britain two years before the launch and employing the most splendid selection of materials. A document that had circulated since before the war, had specified that the third and last *Victoria & Albert's*

FIG. 17.2
Royal Yacht *Britannia* – bridge.

Royal Yacht Britannia

replacement should have a 'well-balanced, graceful and dignified appearance'. No one who has ever seen the vessel in the course of her active career or has visited the *Britannia* at Leith can doubt that this objective was splendidly achieved by both her designers and the Clydeside craftsmen who built her.

Official Statistics of *Britannia*

- Gross Tonnage   5,769 tons
- Length   412 feet   (125 metres)
  Height of masts above waterline:
- Foremast   133 feet   (40.5 metres)
- Mainmast   139 feet   (42 metres)
- Mizzenmast   118 feet   (36 metres)

The top 6 metres of the two tallest masts were hinged to allow the ship to pass under bridges.

- Maximum speed: 21.5 knots (40 km/h)

- Range: c. 2,400 nautical miles (4,445 kilometres)

- During her career, *Britannia* steamed 1,087,623 nautical miles (2,014,278 km)
- Crew (1997): 19 officers and 217 Royal Yachtsmen (plus Royal Marines band)

Postscript

From the curragh of a prince of the early Celtic Church to the last of the Royal Yachts this has been the story of ships that are technologically supreme as well as beautiful. They have battled the elements, sometimes winning, sometimes losing, yet offering a comforting womb-like security. As Libby Purves put it –

A ship is a confined world: a touching little universe that once held crew and cargo safe in a vast and hostile element.

Appendix 1

Preserved Scottish Ships, Maritime Museums and Visitor Centres

Balclutha

Superintendent
San Francisco Maritime National
Historical Park
Lower Fort Mason, Building E,
Room 265
SAN FRANCISCO
CA 94123
United States
Tel: +00 1 41 5–56 1–7000
Fax: +00 1 41 5–55 6–1624
Website:
www.nps.gov/safr/historyculture/
balclutha.htm

Buffel

Ram Monitor built by Robert
Napier & Sons, Govan for Royal
Netherlands Navy 1868
Maritiem Museum 'Prins
Hendrik'
Leuvehaven 1
NL-3011 EA ROTTERDAM
Netherlands
Tel: +31 (0)10 4132680
Fax: +31 (0)10 4137342
Website: www.maritiemmuseum
.nl/website/

Britannia

The Royal Yacht Britannia
Ocean Terminal
Leith
EDINBURGH
EH6 6JJ
Tel: +44 (0) 131 555 5566
Fax: +44 (0) 131 555 8835
Email: enquiries@tryb.co.uk
Website:
www.royalyachtbritannia.co.uk

Cutty Sark

The Cutty Sark Trust
2 Greenwich Church Street
Greenwich
LONDON
SE10 9BG
Tel: +44 (0) 20 8858 2698
Fax: +44 (0) 20 8858 6976
Email:
enquiries@cuttysark.org.uk
Website: www.cuttysark.org.uk

Discovery

RRS *Discovery*
Discovery Point
Discovery Quay
DUNDEE
DD1 4XA
Tel: +44 (0) 1382 201245
Fax: +44 (0) 1382 225891
Email:
info@dundeeheritage.co.uk
Website: www.rrsdiscovery.com

Falls of Clyde

Hawaii Maritime Center
Pier 7 Honolulu Harbor
HONOLULU
HI 96813
United States
Tel: +001 808.847.3511
Fax: + 00 1 808.841.8968
Website:
www.bishopmuseum.org/exhibits/
hmc/fallsofclyde.html

Glenlee

The Tall Ship at Glasgow
Harbour
Stobcross Road
GLASGOW
G3 8QQ
Tel: +44 (0) 141 222 2513
Email: info@thetallship.com
Website: www.thetallship.com

Maid of the Loch

The Loch Lomond Steamship Co.
The Pier
BALLOCH
G83 8QX
Tel: +44 (0)1389 711865
Fax: +44 (0)1389 711958
Email: mail@maidoftheloch.co.uk
Website:
www.maidoftheloch.co.uk

Meiji-Maru

Lighthouse service vessel built in
1874 for Japanese Government
by Robert Napier & Sons,
Govan.

Tokyo University of Mercantile
Marine
2-1-6 Etchujima
Koto-ku
TOKYO
Japan
Tel: +00 81 0 3–524 5–7300

Moshulu

Penn's Landing
401 S. Columbus Blvd
PHILADELPHIA
PA 19106
United States
Tel: + 00 1 215 923 2500
Fax: +00 1 215 829 1604
Email: info@mosholu.com
Website:
moshulu.com/site/main.asp

Pommern

Museifartyget *Pommern*
Pb 5
AX-22100 MARIEHAMN
Finland
Tel: 358(0)1 8–531421
Email:
pommern@mariehamn.aland.fi
Website: www.pommern.aland.fi/
welcome.htm

Queen Mary

RMS *Queen Mary*
1126 Queen's Highway
LONG BEACH
CA 90802
United States
Tel: +00 1 562 435 3511
Email: historian@queenmary.com
Website: www.queenmary.com

Sir Walter Scott

Steamship *Sir Walter Scott*
Trossachs Pier
Loch Katrine
By Callandar
STIRLING
FK17 8HZ
Tel: +44 (0) 1877 376315
Fax: +44 (0) 1877 376317
Email: cruises@lochkatrine.com
Website: www.lochkatrine.co.uk

Unicorn

HM *Frigate Unicorn*
Victoria Dock
DUNDEE
DD1 3JA
Tel: +44 (0) 1382 200900
Fax: +44 (0) 1382 200923
Email: mail@frigateunicorn.org
Website: www.frigateunicorn.org

Waverley

PS *Waverley*
Waverley Excursions Ltd
Anderston Quay
GLASGOW
G3 8HA
Tel: +44 (0) 141 221 8153
Email:
info@waverleyexcursions.co.uk
Website:
www.waverleyexcursions.co.uk

Aberdeen Maritime Museum

Shiprow
ABERDEEN
AB11 5BY
Tel: +44 (0) 1224 337700
Fax: +44 (0) 1224 213066
Email info@aagm.co.uk

Clydebank Museum

Town Hall
Dumbarton Road
CLYDEBANK
G81 1UE
Tel: +44 (0) 141 562 2400
Fax: +44 (0) 141 952 1234
Email: andrew.graham2@west
dunbarton.gov.uk
Website: www.wdcweb.info/
culture/

Glasgow Museum of Transport

A new Transport Museum – the
Riverside Museum – is under develop-
ment beside the Clyde at Glasgow
Harbour.

1 Bunhouse Road
GLASGOW
G3 8DP
Tel: +44 (0) 141 287 2720
Fax: +44 (0) 0141 287 2692
Email: museums@csglasgow.org

Inveraray Maritime Heritage Museum

An Irish iron-built lightship *Arctic
Penguin* and the puffers *Vital Spark*
(ex *Eilean Eisdail* ex *vic 72*) and
Auld Reekie (ex *vic 27*) (see Chapter
7) are preserved at Inveraray Pier.

The Pier
INVERARAY
PA32 8UY
Tel: +44 (0) 1499 30 2213
Email: thepier@inveraray.tv
Website:
www.inveraraypier.com/index.ht
ml

North Carr Lightship

Scotland's last lightship; open
Sundays 12–4 and by arrangement.

C/o South Victoria Dock Road
DUNDEE
DD1 3BP
Tel: +44 (0) 1382 542516
Fax: +44 (0) 1382 542516
Email: info@northcarr.org.uk
Website: www.northcarr.org.uk

Orkney Boat Museum Project

In development at The Hall of
Clestrain.

> Hugh Halcro-Johnston
> Orphir House,
> ORPHIR
> Orkney
> KW17 2RD
> Email: directors@orkneyboat
> museum.org.uk
> Website: www.orkneyboat
> museum.org.uk/

Scottish Fisheries Museum

> St Ayles
> Harbourhead
> ANSTRUTHER
> KY10 3AB
> Tel: + 44 (0) 1333 310628
> Email: enquiries@scotfish
> museum.org

Scottish Maritime Museum

Organised on three sites – the main
museum at Irvine and two comple-
mentary establishments at Braehead
and Dumbarton. The puffer *Spartan*
(see Chapter 7) is preserved at Irvine.

> Harbourside
> IRVINE
> KA12 8QE
> Tel: +44 (0) 1294 278283
> Fax: +44 (0) 1294 313211
> Email: info@scottishmaritime
> museum.org
> Website: www.scottishmaritime
> museum.org/

> Clydebuilt
> Braehead Shopping Centre
> Kings Inch Road
> GLASGOW
> G51 4BN
> Tel: +44 (0) 141 886 1013

> Denny Ship Model Experiment
> Tank
> Castle Street
> DUMBARTON
> G82 1QS
> Tel: +44 (0) 1389 763444
> Fax: +44 (0) 1389 743093

Time Line

c.80–85	The Campaign of Agricola
c.500	Arrival of the Scots in Dalriada
c.500	The *Curragh*
c.597	Death of St Columba
794	Viking raids
843	Kenneth MacAlpin unites Kingdoms of Picts and Scots
c.900	The *Birlinn*
1164	Death of Somerled
1263	Battle of Largs and defeat of Haakon IV
1295	Auld Alliance – treaty signed between Scotland and France
1314	Battle of Bannockburn
1493	Forfeiture of the Lordship of the Isles
1503	Marriage of James IV to Princess Margaret Tudor
1511	Launch of the *Great Michael*
1513	Battle of Flodden
1603	Union of the Crowns
1668	Establishment of Port Glasgow
1698	First Darien Expedition
1707	Treaty of Union
1715	Jacobite Rising
1745	Jacobite Rising
1759	Establishment of the Carron Ironworks
1769	James Watt patents the separate condenser for the steam engine
1770	Golbourne's plan to dredge the Clyde
1773	Voyage of the *Hector*
1788	Patrick Millar's steamboat experiments at Dalswinton
1790	Completion of Forth and Clyde Canal
1792	Outbreak of War with France
1801	Symington's trials of the *Charlotte Dundas*
1812	*Comet*
1822	Completion of Caledonian Canal
1824	HMS *Unicorn*

1828	Neilson patents the hot-blast process for iron-making
1840	PS *Britannia*
1841	Robert Napier establishes his iron shipyard at Govan
1856	The Puffer
1861	HMS *Black Prince*
1869	*Cutty Sark*
1869	Opening of Suez Canal
1872	J. & G. Thomson establish their shipyard at Clydebank
1874	Triple expansion engine developed by A.C. Kirk
1878	First ocean-going steel ship *Rotomahama* built by Denny Bros
1878	*Falls of Clyde*
1883	First commercial test tank for ship design built for Denny Bros
1886	*Balclutha*
1896	*Glenlee*
1900	*Sir Walter Scott*
1901	First commercial turbine steamer *King Edward* built
1901	RRS *Discovery*
1904	*Moshulu*
1906	Yarrow Shipbuilders move from Thames to Clyde
1907	*Lusitania*
1914	Outbreak of First World War
1918	HMS *Hood*
1934	*Queen Mary*
1939	Outbreak of Second World War
1944	HMS *Vanguard*
1947	*Waverley*
1953	RY *Britannia*
1971	End of scheduled Trans-atlantic passenger services from Clyde

A Short Glossary of Nautical Terms

AFT	Near or toward the stern of the vessel
AFTER	Moving towards the stern
ARSENAL	Storage for weapons, ammunition and armaments
ARTILLERY	Guns and ordnance
AXIS POWERS	Germany, Italy and (later) Japan – allies in Second World War
BALINGARS	Small mediaeval ships
BALLAST	Heavy substances loaded by a vessel to improve stability, trim, sea-keeping and to increase the immersion at the propeller. In the days of sail rocks and sand were used. Modern ships use seawater loaded in ballast tanks placed at the bottom of the ship
BARQUE	3-masted vessel with fore and main masts square-rigged and mizzen mast fore-and-aft rigged
BARQUENTINE	3-masted vessel with fore mast square-rigged, main and mizzen masts fore and aft rigged
BASILISK	A large cannon usually made of brass
BATTERY	Emplacement for guns and artillery
BATTLESHIP	Formerly the most heavily armed and armoured warship
BEAM	The width of a ship. Also called breadth
BEARING	The direction of an object (with reference to you, your ship, another object)
BIRLINN	Name for an early Scots warship or galley, powered by oars and/or sail
BLOCKADE	Blocking off on land or the sea-side of a place by hostile forces to prevent entry or exit
BREAKING-UP	The fate of many ships that have escaped storm or defeat in battle
BREAKWATER	A jetty or mole built to break force of waves
BROADSIDE	Discharge of all guns on one side of a ship

BULKHEAD	Transverse or longitudinal partitions separating portions of the ship ('walls' in a ship)
BUNKER COAL	Fuel coal for a steamship
CAPITAL SHIPS	Once an important ship in a navy, such as a battle-ship or battle cruiser. Now refers to aircraft carriers
CARRACK	An old name for an armed merchant ship
CARVEL	Ship built with planks flush. (See also clinker-built)
CHIEF	The crew's term for the chief engineer
CLINKER-BUILT	Ship made with external planks overlapping downwards (e.g. Norse longships) and fastened with nails
CLIPPER	Usually a fast ship with raked bows – that exceeds or clips speed records
COMPOSITE STRUCTURE	In the 19th century a method of ship construction combining wood and iron e.g. the *Cutty Sark* clipper
CONDENSER	Chamber in a ship's steam-engine in which steam is condensed
CONTRABAND	Smuggled goods
CONVOY	Escorting a number of ships, especially merchant ships, by armed force
CRUISER	A large warship of high speed and medium armament (rated according to number and size of guns)
CURRAGH	(Or coracle). An early wicker vessel probably covered with skins and capable of navigating in seas around Scotland
DERRICK	A ship's crane with adjustable arms used for shifting cargo
DISPLACEMENT	The weight of the water displaced by a vessel
DRAUGHT	The depth of a ship in the water. The vertical distance between the waterline and the keel, is expressed in metres except in the USA where it is in feet
DRY DOCK	A basin for receiving a vessel for repairs, capable of being pumped dry (to repair vessel and scrape marine growth from bottom)

EVEN KEEL	Floating level (with no listing to one side or another)
FITTING-OUT	Equipping a new vessel
FLAGSHIP	One which is flying the flag of an admiral, to show he is on board
FOR'ARD	Near or toward the bow of a vessel
FORE-AND-AFT-RIGGED	Sails that are set in the direction of the ship's length (cf square-rigged)
FORECASTLE OR FOC'S'LE	The raised part of the forward end of a ship's hull, taking its name from the days of sailing ships where the forecastle formed a sort of 'castle' on the ship's prow used for defending the ship
FOUNDER	To sink
FRIGATE	In the 19th century in particular, a warship next in size and equipment to the ships of the line. Nowadays a ship smaller than a destroyer
GABBART	A small inshore Scottish cargo vessel in the 19th century
GALLEY	Usually a flat single-decked vessel using sails and oars. e.g. the Galley of Lorne
GROUNDING	Running ashore (hitting the bottom)
GUNWALE	The upper edge of a vessel or boat's side
HALYARDS	Ropes and tackle for raising or lowering sails and rigging
HEAVE TO	To bring vessel on a course on which it rides easily in bad weather or to stop a ship for a particular purpose
HELM	A tiller or a wheel to turn the rudder during manoeuvring and navigation. The steering wheel of the ship
HORSEPOWER	A unit of work for doing work on and with ship's engines
HULK	The remains of the body of a dismantled or abandoned ship
HULL	The basic frame of the ship

15-INCH GUN	A very large and powerful gun, employed by battleships and battle cruisers. Other large guns are similarly measured by the calibre or internal diameter of the gun
IRONCLAD	A ship encased with plates of iron on top of a largely timber construction
JURY (RIG)	Makeshift rig (emergency rig) of the rigging or steering of a sailing ship
JUTLAND, BATTLE OF	Battle in North Sea between navies of GB and Germany in 1917. Indecisive
KEEL	The timber or bar forming the backbone of the vessel and running from the stem to the stempost at the bottom of the ship
KNOT	Speed of 1 nautical mile per hour (1.7 land miles per hour)
LEEWARD	The direction away from the wind
LINER	Originally a ship following a regular route. Later, more specifically an extremely large passenger-carrying vessel
LOGBOOK	A book containing the official record of a ship's activities together with remarks concerning the state of the weather, etc. Also called Captain's Log. A full nautical record of a ship's voyage, written up at the end of each watch by the deck officer on watch. The principal entries might be: courses steered; distance run; compass variations, sea and weather conditions; ship's position, principal headlands passed; and any unusual happenings such as fire, collision, etc.
MASTER	A term for the captain, a holdover from the days when the captain was literally, and legally, the 'master' of the ship and crew
MIZZEN	The aftermost mast of a three or two masted ship
MONITOR	A slow-moving shallow draught warship with specially heavy gun power
MOORING	Securing to a dock or to a buoy, or anchoring

NET TONNAGE	The cubic space available for carrying cargo and passengers
OVERHAUL	Another word for refit or restoration of a vessel in port
PADDLE BOXES	The covers over the propulsion paddles on some steamers
POOP	Raised deck on stern of ship
PORT	Left side or to the left of a vessel. Formerly the larboard
PREVAILING WINDS	The usual or normal winds at any one place
PROCUREMENT	The acquisition of supplies etc. for a vessel
PUT TO SEA	To leave port
RUDDER	Basically a development of the ancient hinged device for steering a ship. The tiller
SAGA	A Norse story in prose
SALVAGE	To save a vessel or cargo from total loss after an accident; recompense for having saved a ship or cargo from danger
SCREW	A term for propeller – at rear of ship and in contrast to paddle propulsion
SCUTTLING	To make holes or open the valves (sea cocks) so as to sink a vessel
SHIP OF THE LINE	The capital ship of the sailing ship era, a ship usually of at least 74 guns which was able to lie in the line of battle
SHIPPING LINE	A company which possesses a fleet or line of ships
SHIP'S TIME	Ship's time was counted by the half hour, starting at midnight. A half hour after 12 was one bell; one o'clock, two bells; and so on until four o'clock, which was eight bells. The counting then started over again, with 4:30 being one bell
SLOOP	A small single-masted, fore-and-aft rigged vessel with mainsail and jib. A small warship
SQUARE-RIGGED	Having the principal sails hung on yards running across the mast, at right angles to the length of the ship (cf fore-and-aft rigged)

STARBOARD	The right side or toward the right of a ship
STATEROOM	A large commodious cabin on a passenger ship
STEERAGE	Formerly the part of a passenger ship allocated to passengers travelling at the cheapest rate
STEM	The timber at the extreme forward part of a boat secured to the forward end of the keel
STERN	Rear part of a ship or boat
STEVEDORES (from the Spanish)	Men employed in loading and discharging cargoes. Dockers
TAFFRAIL	Rail round the stern of a ship
TONNAGE	Cubic or freight-carrying capacity of a cargo ship
TOPGALLANT	One of the upper sails on a sailing vessel
TOPMAST	An upper mast
TRIPLE EXPANSION ENGINE	An engine in which steam is used three times at increasingly lower pressure. The invention of the triple expansion engine and the greater fuel efficiency it produced transformed long distance navigation in the 19th century
TURBINE	Efficient engine in which power is generated by high pressure steam passing through sets of blades rotating within a casing
TURRET	A revolving tower with accommodation for guns and gunners on a warship
U-BOAT	Unterseeboot or German for submarine
VICTUALLING	Loading a ship with stores while in dock
WAIST	The portion of the deck between the forecastle and quarterdeck of a sailing vessel
WAKE	A vessel's track through the water
WHALER	A whaling vessel
WIND-BOUND	Kept in port by off shore high winds from off-shore; embayed

Index

Acadia xix, 58, 60, 67
Admiral Scheer 135
Africa 67
Alasdair, Alasdair
  MacMhaighster, writer 25
Albion Line 37–38
Allan Line 40
America 67
America's Cup ix, 18
Anchor Line ix, 38–41, 120
Anson, HMS 154, 159
Aquitania xiii, 15, 53, 114, 120,
  123, 133
Ark Royal, HMS 134, 155–157
Armed Merchant Cruisers 115
Asia 67
Auld Reekie ex VIC27 182

BAE Systems 2, 18
Balclutha xix, 97–98, 179, 186
Barbarossa see *Britannia*, Cunard
  Line 67
Barclay Curle, shipbuilders 40
Bell, Henry, engineer x, xiii, 8, 44,
  46–47, 50, 52, 55, 161
Birlinn ix, xvii, 6, 17, 21–22, 24–25,
  28, 68, 82, 167, 173, 185, 187
'Birlinn of Clanranald', poem 25
Bismarck 136–137, 155
Black Prince, HMS x, xiv, xix, 8,
  12, 15, 73–80, 82, 160, 186
Blake, George, writer 146
Bloodhound, HMS 74

Blue Riband 113, 116, 120, 146,
  151
Bone, David W., writer 111
Boston x, 40, 55, 60–64, 66, 120
Boswell, James, writer 34, 36
Britannia, Cunard Line vii, x, xiii,
  xix, 1, 10, 54–55, 57–67, 113,
  117, 186
Britannia, Royal Yacht xi, xv, xvii,
  xix, 12, 172–173, 176, 179
British National Antarctic
  Expedition 101, 110
Briton xv
Brown, John, shipbuilders x, xix,
  53, 59, 113, 117–118, 130–131,
  141–143, 150, 153, 155,
  157–158, 172, 174
Bruce, William Spiers, explorer
  101–102
Brunel, Isambard Kingdom,
  engineer 52
Buffel 179
Burns, Robert, writer 81

Caledonia, Anchor Line 39, 58,
  60
Caledonia, Cunard Line 60
California 39
Cambria 67
Cameronia 39, 120
Canada 67
Canadian Pacific Railways 40
Carmania 117–118, 120

Chanticleer 166
Charlotte Dundas 7, 44, 48, 185
Chindit 69
City of Dunedin 37
Clinker-built construction 21, 22, 188
Columbella, HMS see *Columbia* 40
Columbia, Anchor Line ix
Columbia, Cunard Line 43, 63
Comet vii, ix–x, xiii, xv, xix, 1–2, 44–53, 55, 87, 161, 166, 185
Composite vessel 83
Conrad, Joseph, writer 87, 91, 94, 111
Crane, Hart, writer 82–83
Crinan Canal 49–50, 70
Cunard Line 57, 62, 119
Cunard, Samuel, shipowner 10, 54, 56, 60–61, 66–67
Curacoa, HMS 139
Curragh 6, 20–21, 68, 177, 185, 188
Cutty Sark vii, x, xiv, xvii, xix, 2, 15, 81, 83–94, 179, 186, 188

Denny & Rankin, shipbuilders 37
Denny, William & Bros, shipbuilders 4, 10, 59, 83, 87, 94, 118, 163, 165, 171
Deutschland 111, 113–114, 119,
Devonia 38–40
Diamond 6–7, 111
Dickens, Charles, writer x, 63–67, 80
Discovery vii, x, xiv, xix, 101, 103–111, 180, 186
Donaldson Line 40

Dreadnought, HMS 74, 114, 128–129, 155, 160, 173
du Teillay 17
Duke of York, HMS 154, 159
Duncan, Admiral ix, 13
Duncan, Robert, shipbuilder xix, 38, 58–59
Dundee Whalers, song 112

Eilean Eisdeal ex VIC 72 71
Emerald, HMS ex HMS *Black Prince* 80
Emperor 167–168
Empress of Canada 43, 133
Empress of Scotland 43
Etruria 117
Europa 67

Fairfield Shipbuilding Co. 59, 117, 130, 154–155, 157
Fairy, royal yacht 165, 174
Falls of Clyde xix, 99–100, 180, 186
Ferguson Shipbuilders 18
Ferreira ex *Cutty Sark* 90
Fisher, John Arbuthnot, naval officer 74, 128–129
Force H 134–135
Forth & Clyde Canal xix, 7–8, 44, 49, 69–70, 163, 185
Fulton, Robert, engineer 44, 48, 51

Galatea, ex *Glenlee* 93, 96
Gallacher, Tom, writer 1, 10, 140, 150
Geddes, Patrick, writer 104
Glasgow 69

Glenlee vii, x, xiv, xix, 1, 93, 95–97, 99–100, 180, 186
Gokstad Ship ix, 22–23
Great Eastern 75
Great Harry 31
Great Michael see *Michael* vii, 28, 185
Gunn, Neil, writer 7

Hamilton, William, shipbuilders xix, 100
Hawaii Maritime Center 100, 180
Hay, J. & J., shipbuilders xv, 69
Hebridean Princess 172, 174
Hector xiii, 36, 185
Hekla later *Scotia* 102, 105
Helensburgh xv
Henderson, D. & W., shipbuilders 39
Hibernia 67
Hindustan ix
Historie and Cronicles of Scotland, book 30
Hohenzollern 174
Holland, Lancelot, Vice Admiral 36–37
Hood, HMS vii, x, xiv, xix, 1, 15, 44, 73, 128–138, 153, 155, 186
Howe, HMS 154, 159

Impregnable III, HMS ex HMS *Emerald*, ex HMS *Black Prince* 80
Indefatigable, HMS 129, 157
Inglis, A. & J., shipbuilders xix, 161–162
Invereshie 94
Invergordon Mutiny 132

Iona 163, 165–166
Irrawaddy Flotilla Company ix
Ivanhoe xi

Jackal, HMS 74
James IV, King of Scots ix
James Nicol Fleming 38
Jeanie Deans 162, 169–170
Johnson, Samuel, writer 34

Kaiser Wilhelm der Grosse 113
Keith, Admiral ix, 14
Kennedy, Bass, writer 167
King Edward xi
King George V, HMS 137, 154–155, 158–159
Kipling, Rudyard, writer 11
Kirk, A. C., engineer 87
Kirkintilloch xv, xix, 69–71
Kronprinz Wilhelm 113–114
Kurt later *Mosholu* 100

L'Herieux 17
La Gloire 74–75, 78
Lindsay, Robert of Pitscottie, writer 30
Linton, Hercules, designer 81
Lipton, Sir Thomas, yacht-owner 17
Lizard, HMS 74, 131
Longship 21–22, 27–28, 188
Lucania 113, 117
Lucy Ashton 169
Lusitania vii, x, xiii, xix, 15, 44, 113–115, 117–127, 186

MacGregor, P., shipbuilders 69

Maid of the Loch 171, 180
Margaret of Clyde 34
Margery 163
Maria do Amparo, ex *Ferreira*, ex *Cutty Sark* 90
Marmion 162
Mary Rose 30
Masefield, John, writer 139
Mauretania 117, 120, 133
McMillan, Robert, shipbuilders 97
Meiji-Maru 180
Melvill, James C., East India Company official 54
Metagama ix, 40, 42–43
Michael xix, 22, 27–33, 44, 173, 185
Moodie, George, ship master 83
Moshulu ex *Kurt* xix, 100, 180, 186
Munro, Neil, writer 2, 17, 68, 71, 163

Napier, David, engineer 44, 52
Napier, Robert, engineer and shipbuilder ix, xv, xix, 8–10, 52, 54, 57, 59, 67, 73, 75–76, 78, 80, 146, 179–180, 186
Nelson, HMS 154
Nestor 34, 36
Newhaven xix, 28–29, 49
Niagara 67

Pacific Queen, ex *Star of Alaska*, ex *Balclutha* 98
Parsons, Charles, engineer 118, 128
Paul, Matthew & Co., engineers 171

Penn's Landing, Philadelphia 100
Persia 67
Peter Denny 37
Petrel 167–168
Pommern 181
Prien, Gunther, naval officer 133
Prince of Wales, HMS 133
Prinz Eugen 136
Puffer vii, x, xv, xix, 1, 68–72, 182–183, 186
Purves, Libby, writer 91, 177

Queen Elizabeth 2 xix, 12, 150–152
Queen Mary vii, x, xiv, xix, 1–2, 67, 133, 139–147, 149–152, 181, 186
Queen Mary 2 19, 62, 150

Radford, John, pilot 149
Renown, HMS 73, 129–130, 133, 153, 155
Repulse, HMS 73, 129–130, 133, 153, 155
Robert Henderson 37
Robertson, John, engineer 44
Rodger, A. & Co., shipbuilders xix, 93
Rodney, HMS 137, 154–155
Royal Navy 8, 12, 15, 19, 31, 60
Royal Oak, HMS 133, 155
Russell & Co., shipbuilders xix, 75, 99

San Francisco Maritime Museum 98
Saxon x, 72

Saxonia 117

Scapa Flow xix, 15, 70, 133, 135

Sceptre 18

Schwieger, Walther, naval officer 124, 126

Scotia, Cunard Line 67, 75

Scotia, Research Ship ex *Hekla* vii, x, xiii, 101–102, 104–105, 108-110

Scott & Linton, shipbuilders xix, 83, 85, 88, 94

Scott, Robert Falcon, explorer 101

Scott, Sir Walter xv, xix, 150, 171, 181

Scottish National Antarctic Expedition 101, 108, 110

Shamrock III ix

Simoom, HMS 74

'Sir Patrick Spens', poem 29

Somerled, King of the Isles 24–25, 185

Sovereign 18

Spartan 71, 183

Special Service Squadron xiv, 130

Star of Alaska, ex *Balclutha* 98

Steele, Robert, shipbuilder 58, 67

Stevenson, Robert Louis, writer 38

Stornoway 40, 42,

Stornoway 84

Stromboli, HMS 73

Symington, William, engineer 7, 44

Talisman 162, 170

Terra Nova xix, 105, 107–108, 110-112

Thames ex *Argyll* 164

The Maggie, film 72

Thermopylae xix, 15, 82, 84, 88, 90

Thomas 69

Tirpitz 153, 155

Transylvania 120

Turbinia 118, 128

Turner, William R., ship master 123

U-20 124

U-33 133

U-47 133

Unicorn, HMS ix, xvii, 15–16, 181, 185

Vanguard, HMS vii, x, xv, xix, 1, 15, 73, 153–160, 186

Vesuvius, HMS 73

VIC 18 71

VIC 27 182

VIC 32 71

VIC 72 182

Victoria & Albert, royal yacht 174–175

Victorious, HMS 155

Vikings ix, 21–25

Vital Spark ex *Eilean Eisdeal* ex *VIC 72* 69, 71–72, 182

Warrior, HMS xiv, 74–76, 79–80

Watt, James, engineer 8, 46, 185

Waverley (III) xi, 170

Waverley (IV) vii, x, xiii, xv, xvii, 1, 150, 161–163, 165, 167, 169–171, 181, 186

Weld, Isaac, writer 164

White Star Line 114, 116

Willis, Captain John, shipowner 85, 90

Wood, Charles, shipbuilder 58–59

Wood, John, shipbuilder xix, 44, 55, 58–59, 67

Woodget, R., ship master 89

Brainheart

Paraig MacNeil

ISBN 1 905222 31 9 PBK £6.99

- What Scottish slave abolished black slavery in Morocco in the 18th century?

- How did a journalist invent the kaleidoscope?

- What was the name of the first pony-pulled lawnmower?

- Disguised as a Chinese boy, what Scotsman brought tea to the British Empire?

Paraig MacNeil takes a unique and quirky look at the age of innovation, reflecting on what Scottish inventors, politicians and good Samaritans have offered the world, from the steam train and drainage guttering, to marmalade and the light bulb.

MacNeil offers a brief introduction to each innovator followed by a heroic eulogy based on the style of 'Blind Harry's Wallace', the epic poem praising William Wallace's heroic deeds.

The journey into the age of invention is a light-hearted one and lets the reader revel in the inspiring creativity of 50 Scottish men and women. MacNeil successfully and cleverly fuses verbal wit with a short history of Scottish innovation.

On the Trail of the Pilgrim Fathers

Keith Cheetham

ISBN 0 946487 83 9 PBK £7.99

The fascinating, true story of the founding fathers of the United States, their origins in England and their harrowing journey to a New World.

After harvest time in 1621 around 60 men, women and children held a great feast in gratitude to God to celebrate their deliverance and the first anniversary of their leaving England to found a settlement in North America. These people became known as the Pilgrim Fathers. The feast was repeated annually and became known as Thanksgiving. Almost 400 years later, US citizens still celebrate Thanksgiving. But who were the Pilgrim Fathers?

In this account, Keith Cheetham tells of their flight to Holland, their subsequent departure from Plymouth on the Mayflower in September 1620 and the perils that faced them in the New World. These are true stories of tragedy and danger as well as success.

- Over 170 places to visit in England, Holland and the USA

- One general map, 4 location maps of England, 1 of Holland and 1 of New England

- Line drawings and illustrations

- List of names of those who sailed in the Mayflower

(This) is a dramatic tale of courage, religious devotion, determination and strength of purpose. It is also one of great sadness, deprivation and hardship.

(Cheetham) has written it partly as a guidebook for those keen to tread in the footsteps of the pilgrims.

EXPRESS & STAR

A Vigorous Institution: The Living Legacy of Patrick Geddes

Edited by Walter Stephen

ISBN 1 905222 88 2 PBK £12.99

One might get the impression that Professor Geddes is a vigorous institution, rather than a man.

LEWIS MUMFORD

Patrick Geddes was an original thinker and innovator, an internationalist steeped in Scottishness. His achievements included conservation projects in the Old Town of Edinburgh and in London; community development through greening the urban environment; and plans for Dunfermline, Cyprus, Tel Aviv and over 50 Indian cities. Outlook Tower was the 'world's first sociological laboratory'. He pioneered summer schools and self-governing student hostels, used public art to stimulate social change, and established his own College of Art in Edinburgh and a Collège des Écossais in Montpellier.

Too complex to be fully understood by any one person, *A Vigorous Institution* brings together a team of many talents to take a fresh look at Geddes and his place in the world today. Can he still be seen as a vigorous institution in the 21st century? What is his influence on planning policies in the new, devolved Scotland? Why do his ideas resonate still in Japan, India and Catalunya?

Aspects of his life are re-examined in an attempt to understand further his thinking. How much of an anarchist was he? How influential were his home and childhood experiences? Why did he change his name and why – till the publication of this book – was his birthhouse shrouded in mystery?

A Vigorous Institution is full of tangible reminders of Geddes's life and work, but more important is the living legacy; the dozens of followers who are trying to put into effect, in the 21st century, ideas he was pouring forth in his own lifetime.

Think Global, Act Local: Life and Legacy of Patrick Geddes

Edited by Walter Stephen

ISBN 1 84282 079 6 HBK 12.99

Town planning. Interest-led, open-minded education. Preservation of buildings with historical worth. Community gardens. All are so central to modern society that our age tends to claim these notions as its own. In fact they were first visualised by Sir Patrick Geddes, a largely forgotten Victorian Scot and one of the greatest forward thinkers in history.

Think global, act local
Patrick Geddes, *Cities in Evolution*, 1915

Vivendo discimus – *by living we learn*
By leaves we live

Gardener, biologist, conservationist, social evolutionist, peace warrior, and town planner, Geddes spent many years conserving and restoring Edinburgh's historic Royal Mile at a time when most decaying buildings were simply torn down. With renovation came educational ideas such as the development of the Outlook Tower, numerous summer schools and his Collège des Écossais in Montpellier. In India much of Geddes's belief in people planning can be seen, taking the form of pedestrian zones, student accommodation for women, and urban diversification projects.

Think Global, Act Local: The Life and Legacy of Patrick Geddes examines the life of this important man, who in recent years has become almost a patron saint of the sustainable development movement, and the continuing relevance of his ideas and their place in our world, present and future.

The Art of Putting

Willie Park Junior

ISBN 1 905222 66 1 PBK £5.99

'The man who can putt is a match for anyone.' So said Willie Park in 1920. It is still true today. Willie Park's transcendant manual seeks to share the methods which made him 'the best and most consistent putter in the world'. Equipment may have changed and competition become fiercer, but with Park's guidance, you too will have a fighting chance of making that all-important putt.

This guide to putting for players of all skill levels is fully illustrated; covers every aspect of putting, from grip to the lie of the green; and is a clear, concise and detailed guide to mastery of technique.

The Game of Golf

Willie Park Junior

ISBN 1 905222 65 3 HBK £16.99

The golfer in Willie Park Junior speaks out and voices his opinions on golfing equipment and techniques. Straight from the man who brought golf from Scotland to the world comes a comprehensive guide to playing golf that complements the game of players of all skill levels.

Every aspect of playing, from selecting equipment to proper swing and grip, is explained in detail and given beside the opinion and tips of a successful 19th century golf champion. This commentary reveals the finer details of the game and original techniques that can still be applied today. Including a helpful glossary and diagrams and illustrations, the history and art of golf are revealed.

The Ultimate Burns Supper Book

Clark McGinn PBK £7.99

ISBN 1 905222 60 5

Everything you need to enjoy or arrange a Burns Supper - just add food, drink and friends.

Clark McGinn, one of the foremost Burns Supper speakers in the world, presents *The Ultimate Burns Supper Book*. Containing all the information you need to enjoy a Supper, whether as host, speaker or guest, this book is full of advice, anecdotes, poetry and wit.

Includes:

- A complete run through of what to expect on the night, with a list of courses and speeches
- Advice on what to wear
- A section on how to prepare and present speeches
- A list of common Burns Supper questions (and their answers!)
- A selection of Burns's greatest poems, including a full English verse translation of the 'Address to a Haggis'
- Answers your concerns about eating haggis and extols the pleasures of drinking whisky

This City Now: Glasgow and its working class past

Ian R Mitchell

ISBN 1 84282 082 6 PBK £12.99

This City Now sets out to retrieve the hidden architectural, cultural and historical riches of some of Glasgow's working-class districts.

Many who enjoy the fruits of Glasgow's recent gentrification will be surprised and delighted by the gems which Ian Mitchell has uncovered beyond the usual haunts.

An enthusiastic walker and historian, Mitchell invites us to recapture the social and political history of the working-class in Glasgow, by taking us on a journey from Partick to Rutherglen, and Clydebank to Pollokshaws, revealing the buildings which go unnoticed every day yet are worthy of so much more attention.

Once read and inspired, you will never be able to walk through Glasgow in the same way again.

...both visitors and locals can gain instruction and pleasure from this fine volume...Mitchell is a knowledgable, witty and affable guide through the streets of the city...'

GREEN LEFT WEEKLY

Glasgow By the Way, But

John Cairney

ISBN 1 906307 10 5 PBK £7.99

Glasgow to me is the ugly face that launched a thousand quips. If you're born in Glasgow you're born with a sense of humour. It's the only passport you need to get beyond its boundaries. I've gone around the world several times – I don't know if I've held Glasgow in front of me or dragged it behind me – but I've never been far from her in all that time. Glasgow is a working-class city with a heart of gold. It's Scotland's Chicago, with a streak of New York. It may be the ugly sister of Scotland's cities, but it's the one everybody fancies once they get to know her.

JOHN CAIRNEY

Do you love going to the pictures? Live for the season's Old Firm match? Have a 'rerr' singer in the family? Long to dance under the stars in the Barras ballroom? Is your idea of a local hero Lobby Dosser? And who needs Bob Dylan when you have Matt McGinn?

In this collection of personal anecdotes, John Cairney takes you on a tour of *his* Glasgow, introducing the people and places that have shaped it. Full of the humour, tension and patter that characterises Scotland's most charismatic city, everyone will be sure to find a part of their own Glasgow reflected in Cairney's honest evocation of his home city. *Glasgow by the way, but* is the written tribute Glasgow has been waiting for, from one of its most famous sons.

Spectacles, Testicles, Fags and Matches: WWII RAF commandos

Tom Atkinson

ISBN 1 84282 071 0 PBK £12.99

Spectacles, testicles, fags and matches was a ritual used by Servicing Commandos after doing anything they called 'hairy'. It was a completely non-religious act, but strangely comforting.

From the jungles of Burma to the foggy plains of Germany, the RAF Servicing Commandos were the men who kept the most advanced aircraft of the RAF flying. Yet there has been very little written about them. Historians, up to today, are surprised to learn of their existence and astonished to learn of their activities. But without those Units the RAF would have had great difficulty in providing close cover for the forward troops and the fighter planes would have spent less time in action.

These elite Units serviced and maintained, re-armed and re-fuelled, repaired and recovered the front line aircraft on which so much depended, and did it all immediately behind the most forward troops. Fully trained in the techniques of Combined Operations they could land from the seas on any hostile territory and establish new airstrips almost instantaneously. Equipped to be highly mobile, and to defend themselves and their airstrips, they would be ready to service the fighter squadrons within minutes, and service them quicker than they had ever been serviced before.

They are, surprisingly, the Forgotten Men. This is their story told by the men themselves.

Luath Press Limited

committed to publishing well written books worth reading

LUATH PRESS takes its name from Robert Burns, whose little collie Luath (*Gael.*, swift or nimble) tripped up Jean Armour at a wedding and gave him the chance to speak to the woman who was to be his wife and the abiding love of his life. Burns called one of 'The Twa Dogs' Luath after Cuchullin's hunting dog in Ossian's *Fingal*. Luath Press was established in 1981 in the heart of Burns country, and is now based a few steps up the road from Burns' first lodgings on Edinburgh's Royal Mile.

Luath offers you distinctive writing with a hint of unexpected pleasures.

Most bookshops in the UK, the US, Canada, Australia, New Zealand and parts of Europe either carry our books in stock or can order them for you. To order direct from us, please send a £sterling cheque, postal order, international money order or your credit card details (number, address of cardholder and expiry date) to us at the address below. Please add post and packing as follows: UK – £1.00 per delivery address; overseas surface mail – £2.50 per delivery address; overseas airmail – £3.50 for the first book to each delivery address, plus £1.00 for each additional book by airmail to the same address. If your order is a gift, we will happily enclose your card or message at no extra charge.

Luath Press Limited
543/2 Castlehill
The Royal Mile
Edinburgh EH1 2ND
Scotland
Telephone: 0131 225 4326 (24 hours)
Fax: 0131 225 4324
email: sales@luath.co.uk
Website: www.luath.co.uk